A collection of Advanced Data Science and Machine Learning Interview Questions Solved in Python and Spark (part II)

Antonio Gulli

"Advanced Data Science" is the seventh of a series of 25 Chapters devoted to algorithms, problem solving, Machine Learning, Data Science, Spark and (C++)/Python programming.

DEDICATION

To Aurora for the time together buying her shoes when she was five

To Leonardo who picked the cover of this book when he was ten

ACKNOWLEDGMENTS

Thanks to all my professors for their love for Science

Table of Contents

1. Why is Cross Validation important?

Solution

In machine learning it is important to assess how a model learned from training data can be generalized on a new unseen data set. In particular a problem of overfitting is observed when a model makes good predictions on the training data but has poor performances on unknown data.

Cross-validation is frequently used for reducing the overfitting risk. This methodology splits training data into two parts: one is the proper training set, while the other part is the validation set which is used to check overfitting and find the best partition according to some evaluation metric. There are three commonly used options:

1. *K-fold cross-validation:* Data is divided into a train and a validation set for k-times (called folds) and the minimizing combination is then selected;
2. *Leave one out validation:* very similar to k-fold except that the folds contain a single data point.
3. *Stratified K-fold cross-validation,* the folds are selected so that the mean response is approximately the same in all the folds.

The first code fragment presents an example of cross-validation computed with the scikit-learn toolkit on a toy dataset called diabetes. The size of the test data is 20%, the machine learning classifier is based on a SVM, the evaluation metric is accuracy and the number of folds is set to 4.

Code

```
import numpy as np
from sklearn import cross_validation
from sklearn import datasets
from sklearn import svm
diabets = datasets.load_diabetes()
X_train, X_test, y_train, y_test = \
cross_validation.train_test_split(
     diabets.data, diabets.target, test_size=0.2,
random_state=0)
print X_train.shape, y_train.shape    # test size 20%
print X_test.shape, y_test.shape
clf = svm.SVC(kernel='linear', C=1)
scores = cross_validation.cross_val_score(
```

```
    clf, diabets.data, diabets.target, cv=4) # 4-folds
print scores
print("Accuracy: %0.2f (+/- %0.2f)" % (scores.mean(),
scores.std()))
```

2. Why is Grid Search important?

Solution

In machine learning it is important to assess which is the best configuration of hyper-parameters for a learning algorithm. As usual the goal is to optimize some well-defined evaluation metrics. Let us dig those aspects in more details. First let us clarify that learning algorithms learn parameters in order to create models based on input data. Second let us clarify that hyper-parameters are then selected to ensure that a given model does not overfit its training data.

Grid search is an exhaustive search procedure that explores a space of manually defined hyper-parameters by testing all possible configurations and by selecting the most effective one.

The first code example runs a cross-validation on a KNN classifier with 10 folds. The evaluation metric is accuracy. Then it performs a different grid search on a parameter space defined in terms of number of neighbours to be considered (from 1 to 10), in terms of weights (uniform or distance based) and in terms of Power parameter for the Minkowski metric (when p = 1, this is equivalent to a manhattan distance (l1), or an euclidean distance (l2) for p = 2). The whole grid consists in a space of 10 (neighbours) * 2 (weights) * 2 (distances) points which are exhaustively searched by the algorithm via GridSearchCV. The best configuration (e.g. the one getting the best accuracy) is then returned.

Code

```
from sklearn.cross_validation import cross_val_score
from sklearn.neighbors import KNeighborsClassifier
from sklearn.grid_search import GridSearchCV
import numpy as np

#load toydataset
boston = load_boston()
```

```
X, y = boston.data, boston.target
yint = y[:].astype(int)

#grid = 20 x 2 x 3
classifier = KNeighborsClassifier(n_neighbors=5,
        weights='uniform', metric='minkowski', p=2)

grid ={'n_neighbors': range(1,11),
    'weights': ['uniform', 'distance'],
    'p' : [1,2]}

print 'baseline %.5f' \
    % np.mean(cross_val_score(classifier, X, yint,
cv=10,
    scoring='accuracy', n_jobs=1))

search = GridSearchCV(estimator=classifier,
param_grid=grid,
            scoring='accuracy', n_jobs=1, refit=True,
cv=10)

search.fit(X, yint)

print 'Best Parameters: %s' % search.best_params_
print 'Accuracy %5f' % search.best_score_
```

3. What are the new Spark DataFrame and the Spark Pipeline? And how we can use the new ML library for Grid Search

Solution

Spark has recently introduced *DataFrames* (previously called schemaRDD), a new model for data representation which complements the traditional RDD. A *DataFrame* can be seen as a table where the columns are explicitly associated with names. As for RDD, Spark takes care of data distribution across multiple nodes as well as marshalling/un-marshalling data operations.

Spark 1.2 has also introduced a new model for composing different machine learning modules into a *Pipeline* where each component interacts with the others via homogeneous APIs. Let's review the key concept introduced by the Spark ML APIs:

1. *ML Dataset*: Spark ML uses DataFrames for holding a variety of data types (columns can store text, features, true labels and predictions);
2. *Transformer*: A Transformer is an algorithm which can transform one DataFrame into another DataFrame (for instance an ML model is a Transformer which transforms a DataFrame with features into an DataFrame with predictions);
3. *Estimator*: An Estimator is an algorithm which can be fit on a DataFrame to produce a Transformer (for instance a learning algorithm is an Estimator which trains on a training set and produces a model);
4. *Pipeline:* A Pipeline chains multiple Transformers and Estimators together to specify a machine learner workflow (for instance a whole pipeline can be passed as a parameter to a function)
5. *Param:* All Transformers and Estimators now share a common homogeneous API for specifying parameters.

In the code example below a dataframe with `"id"`, `"text"`, `"label"` columns has been defined. Then a pipeline is created. In particular a Tokenizer is connected to a hashing term frequency module, that is in turn connected to a linear regressor. The whole pipeline is a workflow which is then passed as parameter to a cross validator. The cross-validator performs an exhaustive grid search on a hyper-parameter space consisting in two different regularization values and two different numbers of maximum iterations. A `BinaryClassificationEvaluator` is used for comparing different configurations and this evaluator uses the areaUnderROC as a default metric.

Code

```
from pyspark import SparkContext
from pyspark.sql import SQLContext
from pyspark.sql import Row

from pyspark.ml.feature import HashingTF, Tokenizer
from pyspark.ml.classification import
LogisticRegression
from pyspark.ml.tuning import ParamGridBuilder,
CrossValidator
from pyspark.ml import Pipeline
```

```python
from pyspark.ml.evaluation import
BinaryClassificationEvaluator

#create a toy training set and store in a dataframe
# (id, text, label) tuples.
sc = SparkContext()
sqlContext = SQLContext(sc)
training = sqlContext.createDataFrame([
  (0L, "the eagles touch base", 1.0),
  (1L, "matt dillon play movies", 0.0),
  (2L, "touch down at 10", 1.0),
  (3L, "tom cruise and", 0.0),
  (4L, "baseball tournament", 1.0),
  (5L, "angeline jolie", 0.0)],
  ["id", "text", "label"])

# ML pipeline, tree stages: tokenizer, hashingTF, and
lr.
tokenizer = Tokenizer(inputCol="text",
outputCol="words")
hashingTF =
HashingTF(inputCol=tokenizer.getOutputCol(),
outputCol="features")

# build the estimator
lr = LogisticRegression(maxIter=10, regParam=0.01)

# a simple pipeline only one stage
pipeline = Pipeline() \
  .setStages([tokenizer, hashingTF, lr])

# build the parameter grid
paramGrid = ParamGridBuilder() \
  .baseOn({lr.labelCol: 'label'}) \
  .baseOn([lr.predictionCol, 'predic']) \
  .addGrid(lr.regParam, [1.0, 2.0]) \
  .addGrid(lr.maxIter, [1, 5]) \
  .build()
expected = [
  {lr.regParam: 1.0, lr.maxIter: 1, lr.labelCol:
'label', lr.predictionCol: 'predic'},
  {lr.regParam: 2.0, lr.maxIter: 1, lr.labelCol:
'label', lr.predictionCol: 'predic'},
  {lr.regParam: 1.0, lr.maxIter: 5, lr.labelCol:
'label', lr.predictionCol: 'predic'},
  {lr.regParam: 2.0, lr.maxIter: 5, lr.labelCol:
'label', lr.predictionCol: 'predic'}]
```

```
len(paramGrid) == len(expected)

bce = BinaryClassificationEvaluator()

# the crossvalidator takes the pipeline, the grid, and
the evaluator
# run on 2+ folds

cv = CrossValidator() \
    .setEstimator(pipeline) \
    .setEstimatorParamMaps(paramGrid) \
    .setEvaluator(bce) \
    .setNumFolds(2)

cvModel = cv.fit(training)

print "Parameters lr"
print lr.extractParamMap()
print "Parameters cvmodel"
print cv.getEstimatorParamMaps()

# create the toy test documents

test = sqlContext.createDataFrame([
    (4L, "tom cruise"),
    (5L, "played baseball")],
    ["id", "text"])

prediction = cvModel.transform(test)

selected = prediction.select("id", "text",
"probability", "predic")
for row in selected.collect():
    print(row)
```

4. How to deal with categorical features? And what is one-hot-encoding?

Solution

At times datasets contain categorical features. For instance, "Nationality",
can have multiple categories such as "Italian", "U.S.", °British", "French" and
so on and so forth. A one-hot encoder maps a column of category indices into

a column of sparse binary vectors with at most one single one-value per row that indicates the input category index. One-hot-encoding is very useful for dealing with categorical features.

Indeed many learning algorithms learn one single weight per feature. For instance, a linear classifier has the form $wx + b > 0$ and will learn one single weight for the feature "Nationality". Sometimes this is a limit because we might want to differentiate situations where people have more than one nationality (e.g. "French" and "US" might be different from "Canadian" and "US"). One-hot-encoding will naturally capture these types of interactions in the data by blowing up the feature space where each choice of nationality gets its own sparse representation.

In this code fragment a one hot encoding is computed on a toy example by using the new ML Spark library.

Code

```
from pyspark.ml.feature import OneHotEncoder,
StringIndexer
from pyspark import SparkContext
from pyspark.sql import SQLContext

sc = SparkContext()
sqlContext = SQLContext(sc)

df = sqlContext.createDataFrame([
    (0, "a"),
    (1, "b"),
    (2, "c"),
    (3, "d"),
    (4, "e"),
    (5, "f"),
    (6, "c"),
    (7, "d")
], ["id", "category"])

stringIndexer = StringIndexer(inputCol="category",
outputCol="categoryIndex")
model = stringIndexer.fit(df)
indexed = model.transform(df)
encoder = OneHotEncoder(inputCol="categoryIndex",
outputCol="categoryVec")
encoded = encoder.transform(indexed)
for e in encoded.select("id", "categoryVec").take(10):
```

```
print e
```

5. What are generalized linear models and what is an R Formula?

Solution

Generalized linear models unify various statistical models, such as linear and logistic regression, through the specification of a model family and link function. For instance, one formula could be $y \sim f0 + f1$ meaning the prediction for y is linearly modelled as function of the features $f0$ and $f1$. More complex examples can be built by using R operators such as inclusion (+), exclusion (-), inclusion all (.) and others.

In this code fragment Spark 1.5 supports Rformulas for predicting clicks based on an extended linear model which is modelled as function of country and hours. The model is then used to learn from the data via a `fit` operation. This part is still experimental in Spark and will be further extended during the next major releases.

Code

```
from pyspark.ml.feature import RFormula
from pyspark import SparkContext
from pyspark.sql import SQLContext

sc = SparkContext()
sqlContext = SQLContext(sc)

dataset = sqlContext.createDataFrame(
    [
        (5, "ZA", 1, 1.0),
        (6, "IT", 10, 1.0),
        (7, "US", 18, 1.0),
        (8, "CA", 12, 0.0),
        (9, "NZ", 15, 0.0)],
    ["id", "country", "hour", "clicked"])
formula = RFormula(
    formula="clicked ~ country + hour",
    featuresCol="features",
    labelCol="label")
output = formula.fit(dataset).transform(dataset)
```

```
output.select("features", "label").show()
```

6. What are the Decision Trees?

Solution

Decision trees are a class of machine learning algorithms where the learned model is represented by a tree. Each node represents a choice associated to one input feature and the edge departing from that node represents the potential outcomes for the choice. Tree models where the target variable can take a finite set of values are called *classification trees*, while tree models where the target variable can take continuous values are called *regression trees*.

There is a vast literature for modelling Decision trees, however the most common approach usually works recursively top-down, by choosing at each step a variable that 'best' splits the feature space. Different metrics have been proposed to define what is the 'best' choice. Let us review the most popular ones:

- **Gini impurity** is the sum of the probabilities of each item being chosen, multiplied by the probability of mistaken categorization
- **Information gain** is the difference between the entropy computed before and after performing a split on a particular feature, where the entropy of

$$H(X) = -\sum_i P(x_i) log P(x_i)$$

a random variable X is   ;
- **Variance reduction** is the difference between the variance computed before and after performing a split on a particular feature.

In short the space of features is thus recursively explored: the feature offering the 'best' choice is selected and the potential outcomes will generate the children of the current node. The process is then recursively repeated on the remaining features until the full tree is built or the maximum depth for the tree is reached. Once the tree is available, it can be used for classification and/or regression on new unseen data by navigating the three top-down from the roof to a leaf. The prediction is the label of the final leaf. In this image a decision tree for deciding whether today is a good day to play tennis has been presented.

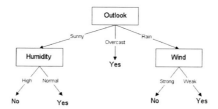

Note that Decision Trees divide the feature space into axis-parallel rectangles organized in a hierarchy and label each rectangle with one of the classes corresponding to the leaf of the tree. Hence Decision Trees can deal with non-linear separable data sets.

Decision trees show multiple advantages with respects to other learning methods such as:

- It is easy to understand why a feature is recursively selected and it is intuitive to understand the workflow represented once the tree is built;
- It is possible to handle both numerical and categorical data;
- It is possible to build trees for large datasets with reasonable robustness for outliers

However there are also limitations:

- Learning an optimal decision tree is an NP-complete problem so construction is based on heuristics which are frequently making locally-optimal decisions at each node. Once a feature has been selected, the decision cannot be reverted (however some extensions of Decision Trees such Gradient Boosted, and Random Forests aim at circumventing this limitation);
- Decision-trees can overfit training data and frequently do not generalize well on new unseen data. Pruning and randomization are the techniques adopted to minimize the impact of this problem.

The code fragment reported below uses Decision Trees for Classification based on the new *DataFrame* Spark representation. Training data is loaded using the SVM file format natively supported by the library. Data is split into training and test with a proportion of 60% and 40% respectively. Then a decision tree is built by fitting the training data and by imposing a max depth of 3. The default split criterion is Gini. Once the tree is available it can be used to predict the outcomes for the test data.

Code

```python
from pyspark.ml.classification import
DecisionTreeClassifier
from pyspark.ml.evaluation import
MulticlassClassificationEvaluator
from pyspark.ml.feature import StringIndexer
from pyspark.mllib.util import MLUtils
from pyspark.sql import Row
from pyspark import SparkContext
from pyspark.sql import SQLContext

sc = SparkContext()
sqlContext = SQLContext(sc)
# Load training data
df = MLUtils.loadLibSVMFile(sc,
"data/mllib/sample_multiclass_classification_data.txt")
.toDF()

# Map labels into an indexed column labels [0,
numLabels)
stringIndexer = StringIndexer(inputCol="label",
outputCol="indexedLabel")
siModel = stringIndexer.fit(df)
td = siModel.transform(df)

# Split the data into train and test
[train, test] = td.randomSplit([0.6, 0.4], seed =
1234L)

# DecisionTreeClassifier
dt  = DecisionTreeClassifier(maxDepth=3,
labelCol="indexedLabel")

# train
model = dt.fit(train)

#predict
predictionAndLabels =
model.transform(test).select("prediction",
"indexedLabel") \
        .map(lambda x: (x.prediction, x.indexedLabel))
```

7. What are the Ensembles?

Solution

The word "Ensemble" denotes a class of methods that generates multiple hypothesis using the same base learner. The key intuition is that the combination of multiple hypothesis learned from the data can indeed generate a better prediction than the one generated with a single hypothesis. There are multiple ways to combine base models.

- **Bagging** trains each model in the ensemble using a randomly drawn subset of the training set. Then each model in the ensemble votes with equal weigh;
- **Boosting** incrementally builds an ensemble by training each new model instance in such a way that the training instances of that previously misclassified models are thus emphasized.
- **Stacking or Blending** combines predictions built with multiple different learning techniques. The combination is also learned with a special ad-hoc learned model.

The winner of a Netflix competition combines different algorithms via blending to provide a single rating that exploits the strengths of each model. In the paper detailing their final solution the winners provide a description using gradient boosted decision trees to combine over 500 different models learned from data. (*Lessons from the Netflix Prize Challenge. SIGKDD Explorations, Volume 9, Issue 2, Robert M. Bell and Yehuda Koren.*)

8. What is a Gradient Boosted Tree?

Solution

A gradient boosted decision tree (GBT) learning algorithm builds in sequence a series of decision trees by fitting the models to the data. Each tree is required to predict the error made by previous trees and then compares the prediction with the true label. The dataset is re-labeled to put more emphasis on training instances with poor predictions.

The key intuition is that each tree is specifically built for minimizing a loss function representing the errors made in previous iterations. Typically the loss function is either a log loss, a squared error or an absolute error. Log losses can be used for classification, while squared errors and absolute errors can be used for regression. In certain situations it has been observed that training GBTs on a slight perturbated sample of the available data can improve the performances achieved by the learner.

As a final note GBTs can handle categorical features and are able to capture non-linearities and interactions in the feature space.

9. What is a Gradient Boosted Trees Regressor?

Solution

GBTs Regressors are gradient boosted trees used to deal with continuous features. In the example below a Spark ML library is used and a training data is converted into a suitable *DataFrame* format. The regressor runs for 50 iterations, which maximum depth is 5. Default loss function is the l2-norm. In this case regression hasve been evaluated by means of three different metrics: the square root of the mean squared error, the mean absolute error or l1-norm, and the r2, a measure of variability for the regression model[1].

Code

```
# gradient boosted regression
#
from pyspark import SparkContext
from pyspark.sql import SQLContext
from pyspark.sql import Row

from pyspark.mllib.util import MLUtils
from pyspark.ml.feature import StringIndexer
from pyspark.ml.regression import GBTRegressor
from pyspark.mllib.evaluation import RegressionMetrics

sc = SparkContext()
sqlContext = SQLContext(sc)

#load a toy dataset with svm format
df = MLUtils.loadLibSVMFile(sc,
"data/mllib/sample_libsvm_data.txt").toDF()
```

---

[1] https://en.wikipedia.org/wiki/Coefficient_of_determination

```
# Map labels into an indexed column labels [0,
numLabels)
stringIndexer = StringIndexer(inputCol="label",
outputCol="indexedLabel")
siModel = stringIndexer.fit(df)
td = siModel.transform(df)

# get the transformed model and split in train and test
[train, test] = td.randomSplit([0.7, 0.3])

# get the grandient boosted regressor
rf = GBTRegressor(maxIter=50, maxDepth=5,
labelCol="indexedLabel")
model = rf.fit(train)

# predict
predictionAndLabels =
model.transform(test).select("prediction",
"indexedLabel") \
        .map(lambda x: (x.prediction, x.indexedLabel))

#compute metrics
metrics = RegressionMetrics(predictionAndLabels)
print("rmse %.3f" % metrics.rootMeanSquaredError)
print("r2 %.3f" % metrics.r2)
print("mae %.3f" % metrics.meanAbsoluteError)
```

10.Gradient Boosted Trees Classification

Solution

GBTs Classifier are gradient boosted trees used to deal with categorical features. In the example below the Spark ML library is used and a training data is converted into a suitable *DataFrame* format. The classifier runs for 30 iterations, which maximum depth is 4. The default loss function is logistic. In this case classification has been evaluated by means of the area under ROC metric[2].

Code

```
# gradient boosted classification
```

[2] https://en.wikipedia.org/wiki/Receiver_operating_characteristic

```python
#
from pyspark import SparkContext
from pyspark.sql import SQLContext
from pyspark.sql import Row

from pyspark.mllib.util import MLUtils
from pyspark.ml.feature import StringIndexer
from pyspark.ml.classification import GBTClassifier
from pyspark.mllib.evaluation import
BinaryClassificationMetrics

sc = SparkContext()
sqlContext = SQLContext(sc)

#load a toy dataset with svm format
df = MLUtils.loadLibSVMFile(sc,
"data/mllib/sample_libsvm_data.txt").toDF()

# Map labels into an indexed column labels [0,
numLabels)
stringIndexer = StringIndexer(inputCol="label",
outputCol="indexedLabel")
siModel = stringIndexer.fit(df)
td = siModel.transform(df)

# get the transformed model and split in train and test
[train, test] = td.randomSplit([0.7, 0.3])

# get the grandient boosted classifier
rf = GBTClassifier(maxIter=30, maxDepth=4,
labelCol="indexedLabel")
model = rf.fit(train)

# predict
predictionAndLabels =
model.transform(test).select("prediction",
"indexedLabel") \
        .map(lambda x: (x.prediction, x.indexedLabel))

#compute metrics
metrics =
BinaryClassificationMetrics(predictionAndLabels)
print("AUC %.3f" % metrics.areaUnderROC)
```

11. What is a Random Forest?

Solution

A random forest trains multiple decision trees in parallel by injecting some randomness into the data, so each decision tree is slightly different from the others. The randomness consists in subsampling the original dataset to get a different training set (bootstrapping) and in subsampling different subsets of the considered feature space in order to split at each tree node.

Once the forest is built, it can be used for classification or regression. In classification each tree predicts a label and then the forest predicts the label predicted by the majority of trees. In regression each tree predicts a continuous value and the forest then predicts the average among those values. In this example a RandomForestClassifier is built by using Gini as a splitting criterion and the default number of trees is 20.

Code

```
from pyspark import SparkContext
from pyspark.sql import SQLContext

from pyspark.ml.feature import StringIndexer
from pyspark.ml.classification import
RandomForestClassifier
from pyspark.ml import Pipeline
from pyspark.mllib.util import MLUtils

from pyspark.mllib.evaluation import
BinaryClassificationMetrics

sc = SparkContext()
sqlContext = SQLContext(sc)

df = MLUtils.loadLibSVMFile(sc,
"data/mllib/sample_libsvm_data.txt").toDF()

# Map labels into an indexed column labels [0,
numLabels)
stringIndexer = StringIndexer(inputCol="label",
outputCol="indexedLabel")
siModel = stringIndexer.fit(df)
td = siModel.transform(df)
```

```
# get the transformed model and split in train and test
[train, test] = td.randomSplit([0.7, 0.3])

rf = RandomForestClassifier(numTrees=3, maxDepth=3,
labelCol="indexedLabel", impurity="gini", seed=42)

# train
model = rf.fit(train)

#predict
predictionAndLabels =
model.transform(test).select("prediction",
"indexedLabel") \
        .map(lambda x: (x.prediction, x.indexedLabel))

#compute metrics
metrics =
BinaryClassificationMetrics(predictionAndLabels)
print("AUC %.3f" % metrics.areaUnderROC)
```

12. What is an AdaBoost classification algorithm?

Solution

Adaboost is one of the simplest yet effective classification algorithms. Its name stands for Adaptive Boosting where a set $t = \{1, ..., T\}$ of simple and weak classifiers $h_t(x_n)$ is used and the classifiers are also used in turn to boost the mistake made by the previous classifier.

Mathematically at the very beginning all the weighs are set to $1/N$, where N are the datapoints. Then at each iteration a new classifier is trained on the training set, with the weights that are modified according to how successful each datapoint has been classified in the past epochs. In particular let us define $\alpha_t = \log\left(\frac{1 - \varepsilon_t}{\varepsilon_t}\right)$ where ε_t is the training error at iteration t, the weights at iteration $t + 1$ are boosted as $W_{t+1} = W_t * e^{\alpha_t} * I(y_n \neq h_t(x_n))$, where $I(y_n \neq h_t(x_n))$ is an indicator function which returns 1 if the output of the base classifier $h_t(x_n)$ at epoch t and for the data point x_n is different from the true label y_n, and it returns 0 otherwise. Therefore the key intuition is that it is possible to decrease the weight of a correct classifier - because it has already solved its task - and increase (e.g. boost) the weight of an incorrect classifier because it still needs to solve the problem for that instance. This boosting is repeated until $0 < \varepsilon_t < 1/2$.

At the end the classifier returns the sign of the weighted combination of basic classifiers $(\sum_{t=1}^{T} \alpha_t h_t(x_n))$. It should be noticed that the base classifiers can be of any type including but not limited to Bayesian, Linear, Decision Trees, Neural Networks and so on and so forth.

In Spark a good implementation of AdaBoost is available as external package AdaBoost.MH, available inside the SparkPackages repository.[3]

13. What is a recommender system?

Solution

Recommender systems produce a list of recommendations such as news to read, movies to see, music to listen, research articles to read, books to buy and so on and so forth. The recommendations are generated through two main approaches which are often combined:

- **Collaborative filtering** aims to learn a model from a user's past behaviour (items previously purchased or clicked and/or numerical ratings attributed to those items) as well as similar choices made by other users. The learned model is then used to predict items (or ratings for items) that the user may have an interest in. Note that in some situations rating and choices can be explicitly made, while in other situations those are implicitly inferred by users' actions. Collaborative filtering has two variants:

  - **User based collaborative filtering: the** user's interest is taken into account by looking for users who are somehow similar to him/her. Each user is represented by a profile and different kinds of similarity metrics can be defined. For instance a user can be represented by a vector and the similarity could be the cosine similarity

[3] http://spark-packages.org/package/tizfa/sparkboost

28

- **Item based collaborative filtering: the** user's interest is directly taken into account by aggregating similar classes of interest

- **Content-based filtering** aims to learn a model based on a series of features related to an item in order to recommend additional items with similar properties. For instance a content based filtering system can recommend an article similar to other articles seen in the past, or it can recommend a song with a sound similar to ones implicitly liked in the past.

Recommenders have generally to deal with a bootstrap problem for suggesting recommendations to new unseen users for whom very few information about their tastes are available. In this case a solution could be to cluster new users according to different criteria such us gender, age, location and/or to leverage a complete set of signals such as time of the day, day of the week, etc. One easy approach is to recommend what is popular, where the definition of popularity could be either global or conditioned to a few and simple criteria.

More sophisticate recommenders can also leverage additional structural information. For instance an item can be referred by other items and those can contribute to enrich the set of features. As an example, think about a scientific publication which is referred by other scientific publications. In this case the citation graph is a very useful source of information for recommendations.

14. What is a collaborative filtering ALS algorithm?

Solution

An ALS algorithm is a collaborative filtering technique which models users and items with a rating matrix R where the entry $r_{ij} = r$ denotes that the user i has expressed a rate r for the item j, either implicitly or explicitly. The problem aims at predicting the missing entries in the matrix or, in other words, it aims at predicting whether or not a user can be interested in a particular item (a movie, a song, a book, a purchase etc.) that was never seen before. This can be achieved by means of a mathematical technique called matrix factorization. The key intuition is that users can be modelled via an unknown latent matrix factor X (each user is a vector) and items can be modelled via another different unknown latent matrix factor Y (each item is a vector). Hence we have two unknown factors to learn and we can do this iteratively. Y is first estimated using the available knowledge on X, and then iteratively X is then estimated using the available knowledge on Y. The alternate least square algorithm (ALS) aims at reaching convergence where the matrices X and Y change very little after a certain number of iterations. This is illustrated in the following image with R being the sparse matrix and X and Y being the estimated vectors.

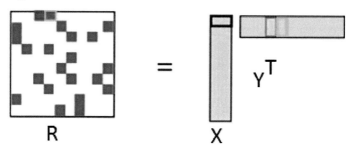

Mathematically, the problem can be seen as a minimization problem of the following cost function

$$J(x_i) = (r_i - x_iY)W_i(r_i - x_iY)^T + \lambda x_i x_i^T$$

$$J(y_j) = (r_j - Xy_j)W_j(r_j - Xy_j)^T + \lambda y_j y_j^T$$

where $w_{ij} = \begin{cases} 0 & if\ r_{ij} = 0 \\ 1 & otherwise \end{cases}$ and λ control regularization. It can be shown that the solution of the above equations is given by

$$x_i = (YW_iY^T + \lambda I)^{-1}YW_i r_i$$

$$y_j = (X^TW_jX + \lambda I)^{-1}X^TW_j r_j$$

and those are the update rules iteratively adopted by the algorithm.

In this code fragment the new Spark ML library is used for providing recommendations based on a user's x item matrix with explicit rating. Then a new unseen user is provided with recommendations for available items. There is a number of hyper-parameters which can be fine-tuned, including the *rank* representing the number of columns in the user-feature and product-features matrix, the *iteration* used during computation, the *lambda* factor used for balancing overfitting with factorization's accuracy and *alpha* which controls the weight of the observed and not observed user-product interaction during the algorithm execution. Note that Spark implements ALS also in the traditional MLlib library based on RDD. In that case ALS has two different methods: one used for implicit ratings and the other one for explicit ratings.

Code

```
from pyspark import SparkContext
from pyspark.sql import SQLContext
from pyspark.sql import Row

from pyspark.ml.recommendation import ALS

sc = SparkContext()
sqlContext = SQLContext(sc)

# create the dataframe (user x item x rating)
df = sqlContext.createDataFrame(
    [(0, 0, 5.0), (0, 1, 1.0), (1, 1, 2.0), (1, 2,
3.0), (2, 1, 3.0), (2, 2, 6.0)],
    ["user", "item", "rating"])
als = ALS(rank=10, maxIter=8)
model = als.fit(df)
print "Rank %i " % model.rank

test = sqlContext.createDataFrame([(0, 2), (1, 0), (2,
0)], ["user", "item"])
predictions = sorted(model.transform(test).collect(),
key=lambda r: r[0])
for p in predictions: print p
```

If there is a need of pseudo-real time updates, then it could be convenient to have a look to the project Oryx[4], which implements the so-called Lambda architecture, where a batch pipeline for bulk updates is used in parallel to another pipeline allowing the faster updates as depicted in this image. Oryx used Apache Kafka and Spark Streaming for input stream processing.

---

[4] **http://oryx.io/**

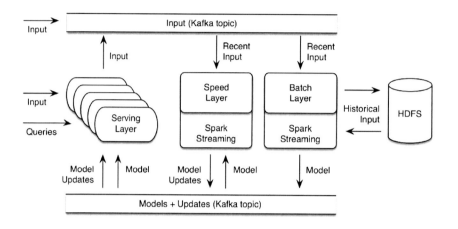

15.What is the DBSCAN clustering algorithm?

Solution

DBScan is a density based algorithm which groups together several closely placed points in a vector space and marks outliers as stand-alone points. Two hyper-parameters ε and $minPoints$ should be provided as input. Points in the feature space are then classified as it follows:

- A point p is a core point, if at least $minPoints$ points are within distance ε of it. Those points are marked as directly reachable from p;
- A point q is reachable from p , if there is a path of points $p1, ..., pn$ with $p1 = p$ and $pn = q$, where each $pi + 1$ is directly reachable from pi ;
- All non-reachable points from any other point are outliers.

At the end each cluster contains at least one core point with all reachable points from it. It should be noticed that a DBScan does not require to predefine the number of desired clusters but this is directly inferred from the data.

In this code example a scikit-lean package has been used to cluster a set of points contained in the diabetes toy dataset with the DBScan algorithm. Spark does not contain yet a native implementation of DBSCAN but this will be probably included in the next releases.[5]

Code

```
from sklearn.datasets import load_diabetes
from sklearn.cluster import DBSCAN
import pandas as pd
import matplotlib
import matplotlib.pyplot as plt

#load the data
diabetes = load_diabetes()
df = pd.DataFrame(diabetes.data)

#explore the data
print df.describe()
bp= df.plot(kind='box')
plt.show()

#perform the clustering
dbClustering = DBSCAN(eps=2.5, min_samples=25)
dbClustering.fit(diabetes.data)

print "clustered\n"
from collections import Counter
print Counter(dbClustering.labels_)
```

16. What is a Streaming K-Means?

Solution

A Streaming K-Means is a version of K-Means where it is assumed that the points are continuously updated in a stream. For instance, we can decide to cluster together new users who are using a mobile phone system and show similar behaviours. In this case not all users are available before the clustering itself because the dataset is continuously updated.

Therefore in the streaming environment data arrive in batches. The simplest extension of the standard k-means algorithm would be to begin with cluster centres and for each new batch of data points reapply the standard k-means algorithm. This is pretty much equivalent to a well-known k-means extension called mini-batch.

---

[5] https://issues.apache.org/jira/browse/SPARK-5226

However two improvements might be used. First, we can introduce a hyper-parameter called forgetfulness which might allow to control (reduce) the importance of data observed long time ago. Second, we can introduce a check to eliminate dying clusters e.g. those clusters which are not updated since long time and probably represent a situation observed in old data.

In this code example the Streaming Support provided by Spark is leveraged (see SparkStream[6]) and new data is processed as soon as it is produced into an appropriate directory. Then each new point is associated with a given cluster.

Code

```
from pyspark.mllib.clustering import StreamingKMeans
from pyspark.mllib.regression import LabeledPoint
from pyspark.mllib.linalg import Vectors
from pyspark import SparkContext
from pyspark.streaming import StreamingContext

# Create a local StreamingContext with two working
thread and batch interval of 1 second
sc = SparkContext("local[2]", "NetworkWordCount")
ssc = StreamingContext(sc, 1)

# continuous training
trainingData =
ssc.textFileStream("/training/data/dir").map(Vectors.pa
rse)
testData =
ssc.textFileStream("/testing/data/dir").map(lambda s:
LabeledPoint.parse(s))

model = StreamingKMeans() \
    .setK(3) \
    .setDecayFactor(1.0) \
    .setRandomCenters(dim=3, weight=0.0, seed=42)

model.trainOn(trainingData)
prediction = model.predictOnValues(testData)
print prediction
```

---

[6] http://spark.apache.org/streaming/

```
ssc.start()
ssc.awaitTermination()
```

17. What is Canopi Clusterting?

Solution

Canopy clustering algorithm is an unsupervised pre-clustering, often used as preprocessing step for the K-means algorithm. The algorithm has two thresholds T_1 and T_2. These are the steps followed:

1. A random element is removed from the set of items and a new 'canopy' is created
2. For each point left in the set, assign the point to the new canopy if the distance is less than the threshold T_1
3. If the distance is also less than T_2 then remove the point from the original set
4. Restart from 1 until there are no more data points to be clustered

Note that each point can belong to multiple clusters. In addition, each canopy can be re-clustered with more accurate and computationally expensive clustering algorithms. Moreover different levels of accuracy can be required for the distance metrics used in 2 and 3. More details can be found in *"Efficient Clustering of High Dimensional Data Sets with Application to Reference Matching, McCallum, A.; Nigam, K.; and Ungar L.H. (2000), Proceedings of the sixth ACM SIGKDD international conference on Knowledge discovery and data mining"*

Spark's community is currently working for integrating Canopy in standard MLLIB.[7]

18. What is Bisecting K-Means?

Solution

The bisecting k-means is an algorithm proposed to improve k-means. The algorithm uses the following steps:

---

[7] https://issues.apache.org/jira/browse/SPARK-3439

1. Starts with all items belonging to the same cluster
2. While the number of clusters is less than k
    a. For every cluster
        i. measure the total error
        ii. Run a k-means on the cluster with k=2
        iii. Mesure the total error after the split generated by k-means
    b. Choose the cluster split that has minimized the total error and commit this split.

The total error can be measured in different ways. For instance it could be considered as the sum of squared error used by normal k-means to assign certain items to the closest centroid.

Spark community is currently working on implementing Bisecting K-means into MLlib[8]

19.What is the PCA Dimensional reduction technique?

Solution

Dimensional reduction is a technique for compressing the feature space and extracting latent features from raw data. The main goal is to maintain a similar structure in the compressed space to the one observed in the full space. The idea of the PCA is to find a rotation in the data, such as the first coordinate has the largest variance possible. Then this coordinate is removed from the data and the process is restarted with the remaining coordinates which are required to be orthogonal to the preceding one. At the end the top k components are retained and, considering the principal coordinates, they provide a compressed representation of the original data still presenting the original structure.

Mathematically let us consider X as a data matrix where the sample mean of each column has been shifted to zero. Then the transformation is defined by a set of p-dimensional vectors that maps each row vector x_i of X to a set of new vectors of principal component scores $t_{k,i} = x_i w_k$, such as variable

8 https://issues.apache.org/jira/browse/SPARK-6517

t receiving the maximum possible variance from x. For the first component we then have

$$w_1 = \underset{||w||=1}{\operatorname{argmax}} \sum_i (t_{1,i})^2 = \underset{||w||=1}{\operatorname{argmax}} \sum_i (t_{1,i})^2 \underset{=}{\underset{||w||=1}{\operatorname{argmax}} \sum_i (x_i w)^2} =$$

$$\underset{||w||=1}{\operatorname{argmax}} ||Xw||^2 =$$

$$\underset{||w||=1}{\operatorname{argmax}} w^T X^T X w = \underset{||w||=1}{\operatorname{argmax}} \frac{w^T X^T X w}{w^T w}$$

where we assume that the vectors w are unit vectors.

For a symmetric matrix $X^T X$ it can shown that the maximum for $\underset{||w||=1}{\operatorname{argmax}} \frac{w^T X^T X w}{w^T w}$ is obtained for the largest eigenvalue of the matrix, which occurs when w is the largest eigenvector.

The problem of PCA computation is then equivalent to the problem of the eigenvalue computation for the matrix $X^T X$. Once we have the first component w_1, we can transform the coordinates $t_{1,i} = x_i w_1$ and repeat the process for the remaining components after subtracting all previous ones. This image provides an idea of what the first 2 components are for a multivariate Gaussian distribution. The first component identifies the direction of the largest variance in the data, while the second one is the second largest variance in the data.

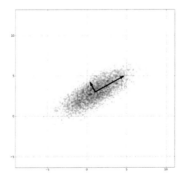

The following code fragment computes PCA using Spark with DataFrames. The first 3 components are thus computed.

Code

```
from pyspark.ml.feature import PCA
from pyspark.mllib.linalg import Vectors

from pyspark import SparkContext
from pyspark.sql import SQLContext

sc = SparkContext()
sqlContext = SQLContext(sc)
data = [(Vectors.sparse(5, [(1, 1.0), (3, 7.0)]),),
    (Vectors.dense([2.0, 0.0, 3.0, 4.0, 5.0]),),
    (Vectors.dense([5.6, 3.0, 1.0, 6.4, 3.5]),),
    (Vectors.dense([3.4, 5.3, 0.0, 5.5, 6.6]),),
    (Vectors.dense([4.1, 3.1, 3.2, 9.1, 7.0]),),
    (Vectors.dense([3.6, 4.1, 4.2, 6.3, 7.0]),),
    ]
df = sqlContext.createDataFrame(data, ["features"])
pca = PCA(k=3, inputCol="features",
outputCol="pcaFeatures")
model = pca.fit(df)
result = model.transform(df).select("pcaFeatures")
result.show(truncate=False)
```

20. What is the SVD Dimensional reduction technique?

Solution

SVD is another dimensional reduction technique based on eigenvalues computation. The technique has a solid mathematical foundation which factorizes a matrix A into three matrices U, Σ, V such that $A = U\Sigma V^T$. It can be shown that U is an orthonormal matrix, the columns of which are left singular vectors, while V is an orthonormal matrix, the columns of which are right singular vectors, and Σ is a diagonal matrix with a non-negative diagonal containing the singular values in descending order. Only the top k eigenvalues and corresponding eigenvectors are retained.

Unfortunately pySpark does not support yet SVD computation while this is available in Scala (October, 2015). Therefore the following code segment shows how to compute SVD in Scala. The Python version is expected to be included in Spark 1.6.X

Code

```
import org.apache.spark.mllib.linalg.Matrix
import org.apache.spark.mllib.linalg.distributed.RowMatrix
import
org.apache.spark.mllib.linalg.SingularValueDecomposition

val mat: RowMatrix = ...

// Compute the top 20 eingenvalues and eingenvectors.
val svd: SingularValueDecomposition[RowMatrix, Matrix] =
mat.computeSVD(20, computeU = true)
val U: RowMatrix = svd.U
val s: Vector = svd.s
val V: Matrix = svd.V
```

21. What is a Latent Semantic Analysis (LSA)?

Solution

Latent Semantic Analysis (sometimes referred as latent semantic indexing) is a natural language processing technique for analyzing documents and terms contained within them. The idea is to build a matrix A where the columns represent the paragraphs (or the documents) and the rows represent the unique words contained in the collection of documents. Then SVD is used to reduce the number of rows while preserving the structure of the columns. Mathematically this process is referred as low rank approximation to the term-document matrix. The original matrix A is generally sparse while the low rank matrix is dense. The low rank matrix has multiple applications. For instance a query term can be translated into the low-dimensional space and related documents can be therefore retrieved. Also terms which are semantically similar will be closer in the low-rank space and this can be used for finding synonyms.

22. What is Parquet?

Solution

Parquet is a common tabular format for saving and retrieving data in Python. Spark supports full integration with Parquet, while SPARK SQL allows to read and write from Parquet files also supporting Parquet schemas. In addition to that Parquet can be used by Spark to implement DataFrame abstractions.

In this code fragment Spark loads an example Parquet file and saves only few fields from the original schema into a new parquet file.

Code

```
from pyspark import SparkContext
from pyspark.sql import SQLContext

sc = SparkContext()
sqlContext = SQLContext(sc)
df =
sqlContext.read.load("examples/src/main/resources/users
.parquet")
df.select("name",
"favorite_color").write.save("namesAndFavColors.parquet
")
```

23. What is an Isotonic Regression?

Solution

An isotonic regression is similar to a linear regression with some additional constrains. In particular this loss function has the following form:

$$(x, y, w) = \sum_{i=1}^{n} w_i(y_i - x_i)$$

, where y_i represents the true labels and x_i the unknown values, with the constrains that $x_1 \le x_2 \le \ldots \le x_n$ and $w_i > 0$. The main advantage of an isotonic fit is that the assumption of linear fitting, typical of linear regressions, is relaxed as explained in the following image. In practice the here present list of elements forms a function that is piecewise linear.

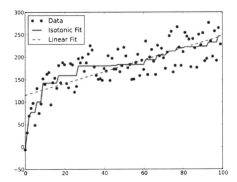

This code fragment computes an isotonic regression in Spark. This code is very similar to a linear regression

Code

```
import math
from pyspark import SparkContext
from pyspark.mllib.regression import
IsotonicRegression, IsotonicRegressionModel

sc = SparkContext()

data =
sc.textFile("data/mllib/sample_isotonic_regression_data
.txt")

# Create label, feature, weight (which defaults to 1.0)
parsedData = data.map(lambda line: tuple([float(x) for
x in line.split(',')]) + (1.0,))

# training (60%) and test (40%) sets.
training, test = parsedData.randomSplit([0.6, 0.4],
seed=42)

# training
model = IsotonicRegression.train(training)

# (predicted, true) labels.
predictionAndLabel = test.map(lambda p:
(model.predict(p[1]), p[0]))

# MSE
```

```
meanSquaredError = predictionAndLabel.map(lambda pl:
math.pow((pl[0] - pl[1]), 2)).mean()
print("Mean Squared Error = " + str(meanSquaredError))
```

24. What is LARS?

Solution

Lars (Least angle regression) is an algorithm for computing linear regression with L1 regularization (aka Lasso). It has been introduced in *"Least Angle Regression. Efron, Bradley; Hastie, Trevor; Johnstone, Iain; Tibshirani, Robert Annals of Statistics 32 (2): pp. 407–499"* Lasso is a shrinkage and selection method that minimizes the sum of squared errors, with a bound on the sum of the coefficients absolute values. If the number of features is very high, then LARS will produce an estimate of which variable to include and what are the weights inferred during the training phase. Instead of providing one single result, LARS can produce a curve explaining the solution for each different choice of the hyper-parameter in L1 which is very useful for cross-validation.

Mathematically: given a set of input measurements $x_1, x_2 ... x_p$ and an outcome measurement y, the lasso fits a linear model

$$\tilde{y} = b_0 + \sum_{i=1}^{n} b_i x_i$$

with the goal of minimizing $\sum_i (y_i - \tilde{y}_i)^2$ and under the

constrain $\sum_i |b_i| < s$ which generally produce a sparse vector of weights. The key intuition of the algorithm is to increase a coefficient of each feature until that feature is no longer correlated with the residual error. Mathematically these are the steps followed:

- Start with all coefficients b_0 equal to zero.
- Find the feature x_i most correlated with y
- Increase the coefficient b_i in the direction of the sign of its correlation with y. Take residuals $r = y - \tilde{y}$ along the way. Stop when some other feature x_j has as much correlation with r as x_i has.4
- Increase (b_i, b_k) in their joint least squares direction, until some other predictor x_m has as much correlation with the residual r.

- if a non-zero coefficient hits zero, remove it from the active set of features and recompute the joint direction.
- Continue until: all features are in the model

It can be shown that this algorithm gives the entire path of lasso solutions, as s is varied from 0 to infinity. In Python scikit-learn implements LARS. An example of coefficients is provided in this image

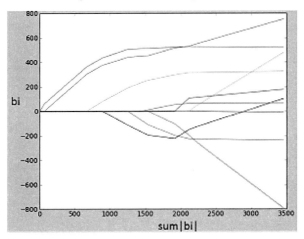

25.What is GMLNET?

Solution

GMLNET is a very efficient algorithm for solving linear regression under the ElasticNet coefficient constrains. It has been introduced in "*Regularization Paths for Generalized Linear Models via Coordinate Descent, Friedman, Jerome; Trevor Hastie; Rob Tibshirani Journal of Statistical Software: 1–22.*" ElasticNet combines LASSO constrains based on L1 regularization with the RIDGE constrains based on L2 regularization. The estimates of ElasticNet are expressed as

$$\hat{b} = \underset{b}{\mathrm{argmin}} \left(||y - xb||^2 + \lambda_2||b||^2 + \lambda_2||b||_1 \right)$$

Spark implements GMLNET as an external package[9]

---

[9] https://github.com/jakebelew/spark-glmnet

26. What is SVM with soft margins?

Solution

SVM allows classification with linear separable margins. However sometimes it could be convenient to have soft-margins in such a way that few data points are ignored and can be placed behind the supporting vectors. Mathematically this is described by using a set of *slack variables* ξ_i which represent how far it is possible to go beyond the margins. The *reg_param in* Spark class `spark.mllib.classification.SVMWithSGD` allows to adjust the strength of constrains. Small values imply a soft margin, while large values imply a hard margin. This image clarifies the use of soft margins with support vectors.

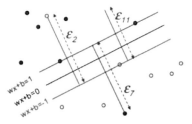

27. What is the Expectation Maximization Clustering algorithm?

Solution

Expectation Maximization is an iterative algorithm for finding the maximum a posteriori estimated in a model, where the model depends on some hidden latent variables. The algorithm iteratively repeats two steps until convergence or until a maximum number of iterations has been reached:

- The expectation step (E) evaluates the expectation of the log-likelihood using the current estimate of parameters;
- The maximization step (M) computes the parameters maximizing the expected log-likelihood obtained during the previous E step.

For example suppose to have two biased coins, A and B, which return head with an unknown bias θ_A, θ_B which we want to estimate. The experiment consists in randomly choosing a coin and perform ten independent tosses for six times (hence a total of 60 tosses). Suppose that during the experiment we don't know the identity of the coins (either A or B) so that we have a hidden unknown variable. The algorithm will iteratively start from some randomly chosen initial parameters (θ_A^t, θ_B^t) in order to determine for each of the six sets whether coin A or coin B was more likely to have generated the observed flips with the current estimated parameter. Then assume these guessed coin assignments to be correct and apply the maximum likelihood estimation procedure to get $(\theta_A^{t+1}, \theta_B^{t+1})$. Note that rather than picking the single most likely completion of the missing coin assignments on each iteration, the EM algorithm computes probabilities for each possible completion of the hidden data. In this way it can express a confidence for each completion of the hidden data.

Mathematically the likelihood function is represented by $(\theta;X;Z) = p(X,Z|\theta)$, where X represents the observed data, Z the hidden latent data and θ the unknown parameters. The maximum likelihood estimate is obtained by

$$L(\theta;Z) = p(X \mid \theta) = \sum_{Z} (X,Z|\theta)$$

marginalizing on Z as   . Iteratively we have that
the following:

- **E-step:** $Q(\theta \mid \theta^t) = E_{Z|X,\theta^t}[\log L(\theta;X;Z)]$ calculate the expected value
  $E_{Z|X,\theta^t}[...]$ of the conditional distribution of the hidden Z given X
  under the current estimation of θ^t
- **M-step:**   find   the   parameter   which   maximizes
  $\theta^{t+1} = \underset{\theta}{\operatorname{argmax}} \, Q(\theta \mid \theta^t)$

EM typically converges to a local optimum and there is no bound on the convergence rate in general. Note that EM should be seen as a framework and specific applications have to be instanced for being applied.

28. What is a Gaussian Mixture?

Solution

A Gaussian Mixture Model is a composite distribution made by k Gaussian sub-distributions each with its own probability represented by $N(\mu_i, \Sigma_i)$ with means μ_i and variance Σ_i. A point of the model can be extracted by one of the sub-distributions. Gaussian mixtures are frequently used to estimate the prior distribution in a Bayesian classification as $p(\theta) = \sum_{i=1}^{K} \phi_i N(\mu_i, \Sigma_i)$ with weights ϕ_i. The posterior distribution can be also modelled as a Gaussian

$$p(\theta|x) = \sum_{i=1}^{K} \tilde{\phi}_i N(\tilde{\mu}_i, \tilde{\Sigma}_i)$$

but with different values $\tilde{\phi}_i, \tilde{\mu}_i, \tilde{\Sigma}_i$.

A typical example of a Gaussian Mixture is topic modelling for documents (also known as Gaussian Mixture Model, or GMM). The assumption is that a document is made up of n words extracted from a vocabulary of size V where each word can represent up to k different topics. The distribution of the words can be modelled as a mixture of k categorical distributions, each of which represents a topic.

This code fragment implements a Gaussian Mixture and it uses EM for training the data. Note that the analytical definition of $Q(\theta \mid \theta^t)$ for Gaussian mixtures goes beyond the scope of this introductive book. The interested reader can refer to the here presented section[10] for a complete discussion.

Code

```
from pyspark.mllib.clustering import GaussianMixture
from numpy import array
from pyspark import SparkContext

sc = SparkContext()
# Load
data = sc.textFile("data/mllib/gmm_data.txt")
```

---

[10] https://en.wikipedia.org/wiki/Mixture_model

```
parsedData = data.map(lambda line: array([float(x) for
x in line.strip().split(' ')]))

k=3

# Build the model (cluster the data)
gmm = GaussianMixture.train(parsedData, k)

# output parameters of model
for i in range(k):
    print ("weight = ", gmm.weights[i], "mu = ",
gmm.gaussians[i].mu,
        "sigma = ", gmm.gaussians[i].sigma.toArray())
```

29. What is the Latent Dirichlet Allocation topic model?

Solution

Latent Dirichlet Allocation (LDA) is a topic model for inferring topics given a collection of textual documents. LDA computes several clusters where the centres are the topics represented as bags of words and the documents are assigned to the closer topics. LDA assumes that documents are generated according to the following rules:

- First, decide on the number of words N in the complete document and choose an initial topic mixture for the document itself (according to a Dirichlet[11] distribution over a fixed set of K topics).
- Then, generate each word w_i in the document by:
  - Picking a topic following the established distribution
  - Using the topic to generate the word itself

Assuming this generative model for a collection of documents, LDA then backtracks from it to discover a set of topics that are likely to have generated the collection of textual documents itself. The mathematical foundation of LDA is outside the scope of this introductory book but the interested reader can refer to this link[12] for a detailed explanation.

---

[11] https://en.wikipedia.org/wiki/Dirichlet_distribution

[12] https://en.wikipedia.org/wiki/Latent_Dirichlet_allocation

Spark supports two learners both based on Expectation Maximization (EM): one is used for offline learning, while the second one for online with mini-batches.

In this code example the data is represented by some word count vectors:

```
1 2 6 0 2 3 1 1 0 0 3
1 3 0 1 3 0 0 2 0 0 1
1 4 1 0 0 4 9 0 1 2 0
2 1 0 3 0 0 5 0 2 3 9
3 1 1 9 3 0 2 0 0 1 3
4 2 0 3 4 5 1 1 1 4 0
2 1 0 3 0 0 5 0 2 2 9
1 1 1 9 2 1 2 0 0 1 3
4 4 0 3 4 2 1 3 0 0 0
2 8 2 0 3 0 2 0 2 7 2
1 1 1 9 0 2 2 0 0 3 3
4 1 0 0 4 5 1 3 0 1 0
```

Then LDA is used for inferring $k = 4$ different topics, each one of which is represented by the probability over the words distribution.

Code

```
from pyspark.mllib.clustering import LDA, LDAModel
from pyspark.mllib.linalg import Vectors
from pyspark import SparkContext

sc = SparkContext()
# Load data
data = sc.textFile("data/mllib/sample_lda_data.txt")
parsedData = data.map(lambda line:
Vectors.dense([float(x) for x in line.strip().split('
')]))
# Index documents with unique IDs
corpus = parsedData.zipWithIndex().map(lambda x: [x[1],
x[0]]).cache()

k=5
# Cluster the documents into three topics using LDA
ldaModel = LDA.train(corpus, k)

# Output topics. Each is a distribution over words
(matching word count vectors)
print("Learned topics (as distributions over vocab of "
+ str(ldaModel.vocabSize()) + " words):")
topics = ldaModel.topicsMatrix()
for topic in range(k):
```

```
print("Topic " + str(topic) + ":")
for word in range(0, ldaModel.vocabSize()):
    print(" " + str(topics[word][topic]))
```

30. What is the Associative Rule Learning?

Solution

Associative Rule Learning is used to mine interesting relations between fields in a large database of transactions. Originally it has been proposed as a tool for basket analysis, where the goal was to report the likeness of buying an item, if a set of items were already bought (For instance buying {*coffee, biscuits*} will increase the probability of buying {*milk*}). Today Associative Rule Learning is used in many online contexts such as Web usage mining, intrusion detection bioinformatics and in many other scenarios where productivity should be optimized.

Mathematically the problem is defined as it follows:

- Suppose to have a set of binary attributes representing the items $I = \{i_1, ..., i_n\}$ and a sext of transactions in the database $D = \{t_1, ..., t_m\}$ where each transaction has a unique id and contains a subset of items.
- A rule has the form $X \Rightarrow Y$, where $X, Y \subseteq I$ and $X \cap Y = \emptyset$ and where both X and Y contain several items
- Let X be a set of items (the so called itemset), and let T be a set of transactions in D and let us define
  - The support $supp(X)$ of X for T as the proportion of transactions in the database, containing the itemset
  - The confidence value of a rule $X \Rightarrow Y$, with respect to a set of transactions T, is the proportion of the transactions containing X and also Y. Mathematically
    $$conf(X \Rightarrow Y) = \frac{supp(X \cup Y)}{supp(X)}$$

The computation of the associative rules requires the user to define a minimum support threshold for finding all the frequent itemsets being above the threshold inside the database. In addition to that a minimum confidence constrain is applied to the frequent items to form the rules.

Finding the frequent itemsets is computationally expensive because it involves creating the set of the subsets of I, which is also known as the powerset of I.

However an efficient way to compute the frequent itemsets is based on *a-priori reasoning*: a set of items is frequent, if and only if all its subsets are frequent. So *a-priori* it is possible to start with sets providing $k-1$ items only and verify, if they are above the support. If they are, the sets of $(k-1)$-items are combined in sets of K-items and the process is iteratively repeated. If they are not, they are discarded thus effectively pruning the powerset. In this example we can see an itemset and a set of frequent items where the red line separates the frequent ones (above) from the remaining ones (below).

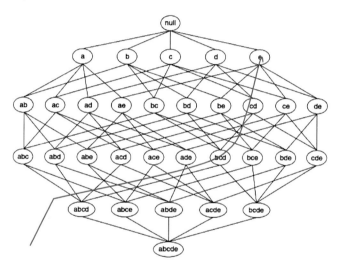

Once the frequent items are available, the confidence threshold is straightforwardly applied to derive the associative rules.

Multiple algorithms have been recently proposed to compute more effectively the frequent itemsets. Sparks implements FP-Growth, a compressed tree based algorithm.

31. What is FP-growth?

Solution

FP-Growth is an algorithm designed for efficiently computing frequent itemsets by using a compressed Suffix Tree[13] data structure for encoding the transaction with no need of explicitly generate the candidates. Sparks implements a distributed version of the algorithm. This code fragment is an example of frequent itemsets in a distributed way

Code

```python
from pyspark.mllib.fpm import FPGrowth
from pyspark import SparkContext

sc = SparkContext()

data = sc.textFile("data/mllib/sample_fpgrowth.txt")

transactions = data.map(lambda line:
line.strip().split(' '))

model = FPGrowth.train(transactions, minSupport=0.2,
numPartitions=10)

result = model.freqItemsets().collect()
for fi in result:
    print(fi)
```

32. How to use the GraphX Library

Solution

GraphX[14] is the Spark solution for dealing with large distributed graphs. This kind of library supports direct, indirect graphs and multi-graphs with the possibility of annotating both nodes and edges. Many graph algorithms are already implemented in a very efficient way. For instance, computing Google Pagerank on 3.7B edges for 20 iterations on a commodity cluster requires

---

[13] https://en.wikipedia.org/wiki/Suffix_tree

[14] http://spark.apache.org/graphx/

about 600 seconds, which is a timing competitive way with specific ad-hoc solutions. Other already implemented algorithms include PageRank, Connected Components, Label Propagation, SVD++, Strongly connected Components and Triangle counts.

In short GraphX is more useful for machine learning because many problems can be modelled as a large graph to mine. Unfortunately GraphX is not yet available via Python binding, although a Minimum Viable Product is expected to be available in Spark 1.6.0. In the meantime users can rely on GraphX via the Scala APIs[15].

33.What is PageRank? And how to compute it with GraphX

Solution

PageRank is a ranking algorithm for web pages developed by Google. In this context Web pages are represented as nodes in a direct graph and hyperlinks as incoming edges in the graph. The key idea is that the importance of each node is recursively split among all the cited nodes. Another way of describing PageRank is in terms of 'random surfer', a model which represents the likelihood that a person randomly clicking on links will arrive to any particular page. This likelihood is expressed as a probability distribution and is mathematically defined as

$$PR(A) = \frac{1-d}{N} + d \sum_{p_j \in M(p_i)} \frac{PR(p_j)}{out(p_j)}$$

The probability of a random walk for node A is constituted by two components. The first part accounts for pages with no outbound links, which are assumed to link out to all other pages in the collection. Their PageRank scores are therefore divided evenly among all other pages. This happens with probability $(1-d)$.

The second part recursively takes the sum of all the in-linking nodes denoted by $p_j \in M(p_i)$, each of which is divided by the number of outbound links on

[15] https://issues.apache.org/jira/browse/SPARK-3789

page p_j. This happens with probability d which is denoted as *the dumping factor*. It can be shown that PageRank computation is equivalent to the computation of the eingenvalues and eingenvectors of a suitable matrix but this advanced topic goes beyond the scope of this introductory book. The interested reader can refer to *"Fast PageRank Computation Via a Sparse Linear System, Algorithms and Models for the Web-Graph Volume 3243 of the series Lecture Notes in Computer Science pp 118-130, Gianna M. Del Corso, Antonio Gullí, Francesco Romani"*

The first code fragment computes PageRank with GraphX in Scala, while the second one computes PageRank via native RDDs definition. The code is included in the Spark distribution itself. The typical choice for a dumping factor is $d = 0.85$.

Code

```scala
val graph = GraphLoader.edgeListFile(sc,
"graphx/data/followers.txt")
// Run PageRank
val ranks = graph.pageRank(0.0001).vertices
// Join the ranks with the usernames
val users = sc.textFile("graphx/data/users.txt").map {
line =>
  val fields = line.split(",")
  (fields(0).toLong, fields(1))
}
val ranksByUsername = users.join(ranks).map {
  case (id, (username, rank)) => (username, rank)
}
// Print the result
println(ranksByUsername.collect().mkString("\n"))
```

Code

```python
from __future__ import print_function

import re
import sys
from operator import add

from pyspark import SparkContext


def computeContribs(urls, rank):
    """Calculates URL contribs to other URLs."""
```

```python
    num_urls = len(urls)
    for url in urls:
        yield (url, rank / num_urls)


def parseNeighbors(urls):
    """Parses a urls pair string into urls pair."""
    parts = re.split(r'\s+', urls)
    return parts[0], parts[1]


if __name__ == "__main__":
    if len(sys.argv) != 3:
        print("Usage: pagerank <file> <iterations>",
file=sys.stderr)
        exit(-1)

    # Initialize the spark context.
    sc = SparkContext(appName="PythonPageRank")

    # Loads in input file. It should be in format of:
    #     URL         neighbor URL
    #     URL         neighbor URL
    #     URL         neighbor URL
    #     ...
    lines = sc.textFile(sys.argv[1], 1)

    # Loads all URLs from input file
    links = lines.map(lambda urls:
parseNeighbors(urls)).distinct().groupByKey().cache()

    # Loads all URLs with other URL(s) link to from
input file and initialize ranks of them to one.
    ranks = links.map(lambda url_neighbors:
(url_neighbors[0], 1.0))

    # Calculates and updates URL ranks continuously
    for iteration in range(int(sys.argv[2])):
        # Calculates URL contribs to other URLs.
        contribs = links.join(ranks).flatMap(
            lambda url_urls_rank:
computeContribs(url_urls_rank[1][0],
url_urls_rank[1][1]))
```

```
        # Re-calculates URL ranks based on neighbor
contributions.
        ranks =
contribs.reduceByKey(add).mapValues(lambda rank: rank *
0.85 + 0.15)

    # Collects all URL ranks and dump them to console.
    for (link, rank) in ranks.collect():
        print("%s has rank: %s." % (link, rank))

    sc.stop()
```

34. What is a Power Iteration Clustering?

Solution

A Power Iteration Clustering is a very fast Graph clustering algorithm outperforming previous state-of-the-art clustering algorithms. PIC takes an undirected graph with similarities defined at the edges and it outputs the grouping assignment on nodes. PIC uses truncated power iterations[16] to find a very low-dimensional embedding of the nodes, but the full description of the algorithm is outside the scope of this introductive book.

The following code fragment computes PIC with 2 clusters for a maximum number of iterations equal to 100.

Code

```
from __future__ import print_function
from pyspark.mllib.clustering import
PowerIterationClustering, PowerIterationClusteringModel
from pyspark import SparkContext

sc = SparkContext()
# Load and parse the data
data = sc.textFile("data/mllib/pic_data.txt")
similarities = data.map(lambda line: tuple([float(x)
for x in line.split(' ')]))

numClusters = 2
maxIteration = 100
```

---

[16] https://en.wikipedia.org/wiki/Power_iteration

```
# Cluster the data into two classes using
PowerIterationClustering
model = PowerIterationClustering.train(similarities,
numClusters, maxIteration)

model.assignments().foreach(lambda x: print(str(x.id) +
" -> " + str(x.cluster)))
```

35. What is a Perceptron?

Solution

A Perceptron is a binary classifier which allows linear separation of data. Like many linear predictors it learns a set of weights w and the output $f(x)$ is a linear combination of the input x and the set of learned weights. Mathematically this is defined as $f(x) = \begin{cases} 1 & wx + b > 0 \\ 0 & o.w. \end{cases}$, where b is the intercept representing a bias in the decision which shifts the decision boundary but not its direction.

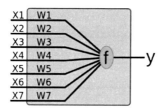

Learning the appropriate set of weights is very simple. At the beginning a random positive choice is made w_0, then- iteratively- the value $y_t = f(w_t x)$ is computed at step t and the weights are updated according to the rule $w_{t+1} = w_t + \alpha (d - y_t)x$, where $\alpha > 0$ is a parameter known as the learning rate and d is the expected true value in a supervised learning setting.

It can be shown that the perceptron converges to a local optimum if the data is linearly separable. The interest for the Perceptron is historical because it has been one of the first machine learning algorithms invented back in 50-ies and, at that times, an ad-hoc computer was developed: the *Mark I Perceptron* a two-layer perceptron still only able to separate linear data. However back in 1990, Hecht-Nielsen showed that a 3-layer perceptron was able to solve non linear separation problems opening the route to modern *Deep Learning*, a state-of-the-art learning technique used with success in many different contexts. Perceptrons and the related artificial neural networks (ANN) were not considered interesting for many years until the back-propagation algorithm was presented in 1986 (actually re-discovered, because the original proposal was in 1974). Back propagation is a form of gradient descent which caused the initial big step for the rebirth of ANNs. The interested reader can have a look to this paper "*Learning representations by back-propagating errors*".*Nature 323 (6088): 533–536, Rumelhart, David E.; Hinton, Geoffrey E.; Williams, Ronald J. °*.

36. What is an ANN (Artificial Neural Network)?

Solution

Artificial neural networks are machine learning techniques inspired by the mammals' brain which is typically organized in multiple layers of neurons. Each neuron has several input layers (with multiple axons), an intermediate layer (synapse), and the output layer (with multiple dendrites). Synapses can modify themselves according to the signal they receives as input. The total input to a neuron is the sum of all the synaptic weighted inputs and the neuron adopts a "all or nothing" firing scheme where the output is not produced until a given threshold level has been reached. Once the neuron has fired, a certain amount of time should be waited before the next fire will happen. Our brain works by following this "simple" mechanism where billions of neurons are working in parallel and continuously getting inputs from other neurons and firing according to their internal state. At least this is what we understood so far!

Now, Artificial Neural Networks follow a similar model where typically we have three-four interconnected layers of artificial neurons. When there are more than 10 layers, then the network is considered as a *Deep Learning* network, a frequently used buzzword in these days. Each layer has an activation function which can be linear or non linear. This image represents a typical ANN with an input layer, an hidden intermediate layer, and an output layer. Neural networks with multiple hidden layers are very common as we will see in the next questions.

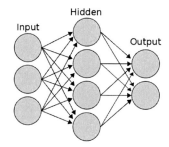

37.What are the activation functions?

Solution

Each internal node in an ANN behaves according to a pre-defined activation function. There are linear and non-linear activation functions and all of them fire after a given threshold level has been reached as described in this image

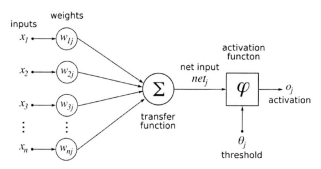

- **Stepwise activation** function $\varphi(x) = \begin{cases} 1 & \Sigma > \theta_j \\ 0 & ow \end{cases}$
- **Linear activation** $\varphi(x) = wx + b$
- **Non linear rectifier** $\varphi(x) = max\{0, x\}$
- **Log-sigmoid,** the well-known continuous and non-linear function

$(t) = \dfrac{1}{1 + e^{-\beta t}}$, with β as slope parameter. One advantage of a log-sigmoid is that the derivative is easy to compute $\dfrac{d\sigma(t)}{dt} = \sigma(t)(1 - \sigma(t))$

- **Tan-sigmoid,** defined as $\sigma(t) = \tanh(t) = \dfrac{e^t - e^{-t}}{e^t + e^{-t}}$. It can be proven that $\dfrac{d\sigma(t)}{dt} = 1 - \tanh(t)^2$

- **Soft-max,** a generalization of the logistic function which squashes a k-dimensional vector z of real values into a k-dimensional vector $\sigma(z)$ of

$$\sigma_j(z) = \frac{e^{z_j}}{\sum_i e^{z_i}}$$

real values in the range (0, 1). Mathematically, .
It can be proven that the derivative is easily computed as $\dfrac{d\sigma_j(z)}{dz_i} = \sigma_j(\delta_{ij} - \sigma_i)$ where δ_{ij} is the Kronecker Delta[17]

- **Cross entropy** is defined as $C = -\sum_j d_j \log(p_j)$ where d_j represents the target probability for output unit j and p_j is the probability output for j after applying the activation function.

38. How many types of Neural Networks are known?

ANNs have multiple basic shapes which can be combined to create sophisticate models. Combining the basic shapes is an art which has been subject of active research in the past years. Let's start from the simplest form of ANN, the **feed forward systems** which are depicted in the image

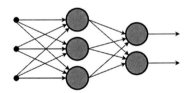

Then there are **recurrent systems** where the output might be recursively used as additional input. A typical model is shown in the image

[17] https://en.wikipedia.org/wiki/Kronecker_delta

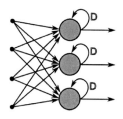

Many more models have been proposed including: **Radial-basis,** where the activation function is typically a Gaussian Kernel, **Hopfiled Networks,** where the activation function is a sigmoid and a concept of network energy is adopted, **Self-Organized Maps,** where groups of neurons appear to organize into specific regions, **Competitive Models,** where neurons compete to learn a model and **Bolzman Machines,** where the input data distribution is compared to the output data distribution.

39.How to train a Neural Network

Solution

Training an ANN can be performed in a supervised or unsupervised manner. One common way is to use the Gradient Descent - frequently in its Stochastic variant (SDG) - which has been revamped by Google for large distributed dataset computations (*Large Scale Distributed Deep Networks Jeffrey Dean, Greg S. Corrado, Rajat Monga, Kai Chen, Matthieu Devin, Quoc V. Le, Mark Z. Mao, Marc'Aurelio Ranzato, Andrew Senior, Paul Tucker, Ke Yang, and Andrew Y. Ng*)

Another common variant is Back propagation (**Backprop**) which passes error signals backwards through the network during training to update the weights with the goal of minimizing a well-chosen error function. Backprop consists in reality of two steps. First, the output is worked out considering the input and the current weights in a feed-forward manner, and then the error is sent in the opposite direction, thus realizing a proper backprop step. In this context the *learning rate* is a training parameter that controls the size of weights and the bias changes in learning. The *momentum* is another parameter which simply adds a fraction of the previous weight update to the current one during the training phase. The momentum parameter forces the search for local optimum to take into account its movement from the previous iteration.

40. Which are the possible ANNs applications?

Solution

ANNs have been successfully used to tackle many learning problems including but not limited to:

- **Data compression,** where the complex representation of the input layers is embedded in a more compact representation still preserving the original structure to certain extents;
- **Patter Recognition** with Optical Character Recognition (OCR), intrusion detection for security, and fraudulent card transaction;
- **Function approximation,** where ANNs are required to fit a given analytical function;
- **Function optimization,** where ANNs are required to minimize a given analytical function;
- **Recommendation and Clustering** with items recommendations and self-organizing maps;
- **Feature detection in Image** with face recognition and disease detections with X-rays;
- **Series detection** with prediction of temporal events such as the future evolution of stock prices and many types of meteorological events;
- **Classification and Regression,** two typical machine learning classes of application.

41. Can you code a simple ANNs in Python?

Solution

In this simple code fragment we are aiming at predicting the vector $out = [0, 0, 1, 1]$ given the three inputs $in = \{[0, 0, 1, 1], [0,1,0,1], [1, 1, 1, 1]\}$. The network uses a nonlinear sigmoid function. At the beginning the weights are assigned randomly. Then for 1000 iterations the output is updated in forward propagation, followed by an evaluation of the error and by a backprop step which updates the weights considering the slope of the evaluated sigmoid at the error output times.

Code

```python
import numpy as np

# sigmoid function
def sigmoid(x,deriv=False):
    if(deriv==True):
        return x*(1-x)
    return 1/(1+np.exp(-x))

# input
X = np.array([  [0,0,1],
    [0,1,1],
    [1,0,1],
    [1,1,1] ])

# output
y = np.array([[0,0,1,1]]).T

np.random.seed(1)

# initialize weights randomly with mean 0
syn0 = 2*np.random.random((3,1)) - 1
l0 = X

 # for 1000 epochs
for iter in xrange(1000):

# forward propagation
    l1 = sigmoid(np.dot(l0,syn0))

    # error
    l1_error = y - l1
    # multiply error by the
    # slope of the sigmoid evaluated at l1
    l1_delta = l1_error * sigmoid(l1,True)
    # update weights
    syn0 += np.dot(l0.T,l1_delta)

print "Output After Training:"
print l1
```

42. What support has Spark for Neural Networks?

Solution

Spark is starting to provide support for ANNs and in particular the first integration with Python is supposed to happen since version 1.6.0[18]. In particular the new ML library supports a Multilayer Perceptron used for classification (**MLPC**). The shape of the network is such that each layer has a sigmoid activation function and the output layer has a softmax activation function.

The following code fragment works only on very recent Spark versions (>1.6.X) and it is based on an internal distributed matrix computation on DataFrames. MLPC uses backpropagation for learning the model together with logistic losses and L-BFGS,[19] an advanced function optimization method outside the scope of this introductive book.

Code

```
# Multilayer perceptron for classification
# it workds with >1.6.X

from pyspark.mllib.linalg import Vectors
from pyspark import SparkContext
from pyspark.sql import SQLContext

sc = SparkContext()
sqlContext = SQLContext(sc)

df = sqlContext.createDataFrame([
    (0.0, Vectors.dense([0.0, 0.0])),
    (1.0, Vectors.dense([0.0, 1.0])),
    (1.0, Vectors.dense([1.0, 0.0])),
    (0.0, Vectors.dense([1.0, 1.0]))], ["label",
"features"])
```

---

[18] At the end of October 2016 it will be possible to play with "night builds": https://cwiki.apache.org/confluence/display/SPARK/Useful+Developer+Tools #UsefulDeveloperTools-NightlyBuilds and the related documentation available online http://people.apache.org/~pwendell/spark-nightly/spark-master-docs/latest/

[19] https://en.wikipedia.org/wiki/Limited-memory_BFGS

```
mlp = MultilayerPerceptronClassifier(maxIter=100,
layers=[2, 5, 2], blockSize=1, seed=11)
model = mlp.fit(df)
print model.layers
print model.weights.size
testDF = sqlContext.createDataFrame([
(Vectors.dense([1.0, 0.0]),),
(Vectors.dense([0.0, 0.0]),)], ["features"])
model.transform(testDF).show()
```

43.What is Deep Learning?

Solution

Deep Learning is a buzzword which entered the mainstream thanks to some recent results capturing the attention of a global audience. Google's Brain project learns to find cats in videos, Facebook recognizes faces in images, Baidu recognizes visual shapes and objects, and both Baidu and Microsoft use deep learning for speech recognition. Apart from buzzwords, the most prestigious minds are world-wide working in deep learning including Jeff Dean (Google), Yann LeCun(Facebook), Andrew Ng(Baidu).

One very interesting progress made with Deep Learning is the possibility to learn how to extract discriminative features in an automatic way. Traditional machine learning requires a lot of human effort for hand-crafting features and machine learning was essentially a way to learn weights for balancing those features.

The automatic discovering of discriminative features is a big step forward toward reasoning. Machines can now learn what is important and what is not, while before humans had to pick features which were potentially important and then let the machines weight them at the risk of missing discriminative and fundamental information simply because it was not considered.

In short we can say that now we have the so called Trainable Feature Extractors and Trainable Learning while before we only had the former ones. Auto-encoders are one tool used by Deep Learning for finding useful features for representing an input distribution.

Another interesting characteristic of Deep Learning is the ability to learn from mostly unlabelled data in a typical semi-supervised learning setting where a very large number of training examples are not having complete and correct true labels.

Yet another interesting trait of Deep Learning is the ability to learn how to approximate highly varying functions, which happens when a piecewise approximation (with constant or linear pieces) of a function requires a very large number of pieces.

Deep learning uses a cascade of many layers of non-linear processing units, which perform feature extraction and transformation. What is still required is to manually compose the layers according the specific problem to be solved. So the big next step would be to learn how to self-organize layers. Typically Deep Learning composes many (recurrent) layers of ANNs with even more sophisticated generative models such as Deep Belief Networks and Deep Bolzmann Machines.

One fundamental assumption is that each following level will learn more abstract concepts of the previous one. This concept is well explained in this image where the first layer learns basic features, while the second layer learns components of human face, and the third layer learns different types of faces. Hence, the learning system is a high dimensional entity able to discriminate many observed features that are related by unknown statistical relations. Learning is thus distributed in the sense that knowledge itself is not associated with one single neuron but it is the result of sharing information within the network and the consequent activation of multiple neurons.

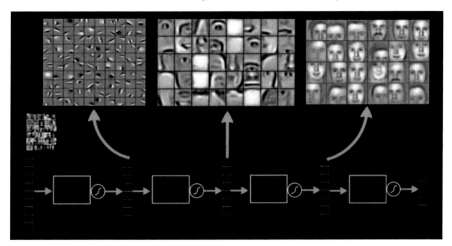

As shown in this image, features become more extended and complex the deeper we go in the network. In addition to that multiple networks can be specialized in different concepts and learn how faces, cars, elephants and chairs are visualized.

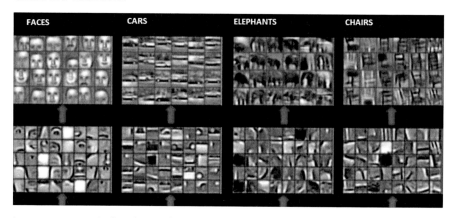

Improvements in hardware have also been an important enabling factor for Deep Learning. In particular powerful graphics processing units (GPUs) are highly suited for matrix and vector operations involved in machine learning and GPUs can speed up training algorithms by orders of magnitude, bringing running times of weeks back to few hours. This allows to increase the number of layers in a deep network and therefore the level of sophistication in representing models. This image gives another idea of how different levels are progressively learning more and more complex visual features.

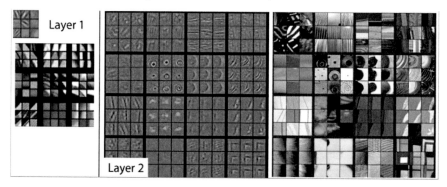

Deep Learning networks are typically trained via backpropagation where weights are updated via Stochastic Gradient Descent using an equation such as

$$w^{(t+1)}_{ij} = w^{(t)}_{ij} + \eta \frac{\partial C}{\partial w_{ij}}$$

so that the weight between the units i, j is updated at time $t + 1$ based on the weight available at time t plus a fraction of the partial derivative of a chosen cost function. η is the learning rate. Google built an Asynchronous Distributed Stochastic Gradient Descent server where more than 16000 CPUs independently update the gradient weights for learning the rather sophisticate recognition of the concept of "cats" from a generic YouTube video. Other types of training have been proposed including forward propagation and forward-backward propagation for Restricted Bolzmann Machines and for Recurrent Networks.

Another rather sophisticate approach uses Convolutional networks (networks where the same weight is used in all the spatial locations in the layer) with 24 layers for annotating images with concepts showing an impressive 6.6% error rate at top 5 results, which is a competitive result with the human brain (*ImageNet Classification with Deep Convolutional Neural Networks, Krizhevsky, Alex*)

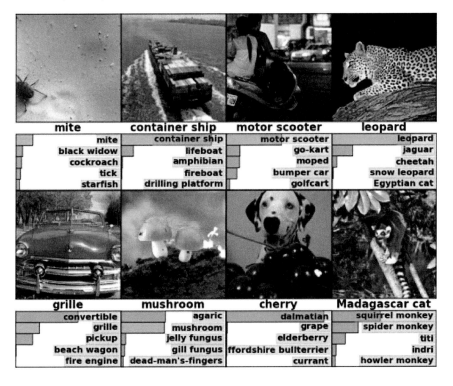

Embedding is another key concept introduced by Deep Learning. Embedding is used to avoid the problems encountered by learning with sparse data. For instance we can extract words from documents and then create "words embeddings" where words are simply grouped together if they occur within a chosen text window. A word embedding $W:words{\rightarrow}R^n$: is a parameterized function mapping words in some language to high-dimensional vectors (perhaps 200 to 500 dimensions). Embedding vectors trained for language modelling tasks have very interesting proprieties where it is possible to express concepts and equivalences such as the relations between capitals and countries, and the relation between the queen and the king, and the meaning of superlative (*"Efficient Estimation of Word Representations in Vector Space, Tomas Mikolov)*

$$E(Rome) - E(Italy) \simeq E(berlin) - E(Germany)$$

$$E(hotter) - E(hot) + E(big) \simeq E(bigger)$$

$$E(queen) - E(woman) + E(man) \simeq E(king$$

This table describes a word embedding learned on a skip model trained on 783M words with 300 dimensionalities

Relationship	Example 1	Example 2	Example 3
France - Paris	Italy: Rome	Japan: Tokyo	Florida: Tallahassee
big - bigger	small: larger	cold: colder	quick: quicker
Miami - Florida	Baltimore: Maryland	Dallas: Texas	Kona: Hawaii
Einstein - scientist	Messi: midfielder	Mozart: violinist	Picasso: painter
Sarkozy - France	Berlusconi: Italy	Merkel: Germany	Koizumi: Japan
copper - Cu	zinc: Zn	gold: Au	uranium: plutonium
Berlusconi - Silvio	Sarkozy: Nicolas	Putin: Medvedev	Obama: Barack
Microsoft - Windows	Google: Android	IBM: Linux	Apple: iPhone
Microsoft - Ballmer	Google: Yahoo	IBM: McNealy	Apple: Jobs
Japan - sushi	Germany: bratwurst	France: tapas	USA: pizza

If you are interested in knowing more about Deep Learning, then it could be worth having a look to a very exciting keynote by the way of Andrew Ng[20]. The author of this book strongly believes that the next step for Deep Learning is to integrate progress in HPC computation (where Spark is) with GPU

---

[20] http://www.ustream.tv/recorded/60113824

computation (where packages like Theano and Lasagne are). This will open the root on deep learning cloud computation by also leveraging the power of GPU platforms like CUDA.[21]

44. What are autoencoders and stacked autoencoders?

Solution

An encoder is a function $y = f_{W,b}(x)$ which transforms the input vector x in the output y where W is a weight matrix and b is an offset vector. A decoder is an inverse function which tries to reconstruct the original vector x from y. An auto-encoder tries to reconstruct the original input by minimizing the error during the reconstruction process. There are two major variants for auto-encoding: Sparse auto-encoders force sparsity by using L1 regularization, while de-noising autoencoders stochastically corrupt inputs with some form of randomization.

Mathematically a stochastic mapping transforms the input vector x into a noisy vector $\tilde{x}$ which is then transformed into an hidden representation $y = f_{W,b}(\tilde{x}) = s(W\tilde{x} + b)$. The reconstruction phase is via a decoder $z = f_{W,b}(y)$ where an error minimization algorithm is used via either a squared error loss or a cross-entropy loss. Autoencoders typically use a hidden layer which acts as a bottleneck that compresses data as in the following image.

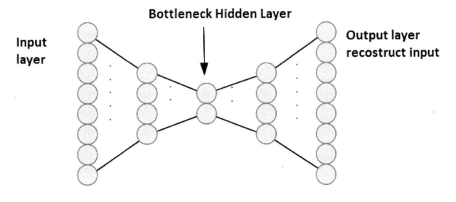

Bottleneck Hidden Layer

Input layer

Output layer recostruct input

---

[21] http://www.nvidia.com/object/cuda_home_new.html

In a deep learning context, multiple auto-encoders are stacked for producing a final denoised output. The "magic" outcome of this combination is that autoencoders learn how to extract meaningful features from noise data with no need of a hand-craft features' selection.

There are also additional applications. For instance, deep autoencoders are able to map images into compressed vectors with small dimensionality and this can be useful for searching images by image similarity. Plus, Deep autoencoders can map words into small dimension vectors and this is a useful process in a distributed topic modellingacross a collection of documents.

45.What are convolutional neural networks?

Solution

Convolutional networks are typically used for multimedia processing and consist in multiple layers of different types:

- **Convolutional:** convolutional layers consist in a rectangular grid of neurons. Also the previous layer is required to be a rectangular grid of neurons. Each neuron of the current layer takes the same weight from the rectangular section of the previous layer. This process is called image convolution. From the Latin *convolvere*, "to convolve" means *to roll together*;
- **Max-Pooling:** max-pooling takes a rectangular block from the convolution layer as an input and produces a single output either computing the maximum, or via a learned linear combination;
- **Fully connected:** *fully connected* are typically the last stage of a Convolutional Network where all the previous stages are connected to a final neuron, which contains all the high-level "concepts" learned so far.

This image represents a typical ConvNet with multiple layers

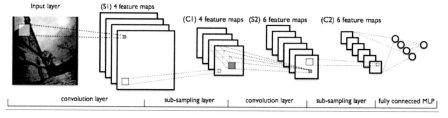

During 2014, Google presented GoogLeNet (*Going Deeper with Convolutions, Christian Szegedy et al.*) a convnet which won an international competition for detecting and labeling photos. As discussed, GoogLeNet scores a 6.65% error rate, which is close to the human labelling error rate. The efficacy of convolutional nets in image recognition is one of the main reasons why the world has shown interest to deep learning. They are driving major innovations in machine vision, which has been used for self-driving cars, drones, robotics and treatments for the visually impaired. The interested reader can also take a look to this very interesting online course from Stanford[22] and an hands-on introduction to convnet presented here.[23]

46. What are Restricted Boltzmann Machines, Deep Belief Networks and Recurrent networks?

Solution

Restricted Boltzmann Machine (RBMs) is a stochastic neural network, where each neuron has some random behavior when activated. The machine consists of one layer of visible neurons and one layer of hidden units. All units in each layer have no connections among each other (as for the non-restricted version) and are connected to all other units in other layer. Connections are bidirectional and symmetric. During training and networks usag, information flows in both directions with same weights in both directions. Training is typically unsupervised, during one iteration the weights are updated in the hidden units and then aiming at reconstructing the visible units with maximum likelihood for training data.

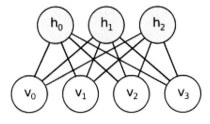

22 https://cs231n.github.io

23 http://danielnouri.org/notes/2014/12/17/using-convolutional-neural-nets-to-detect-facial-keypoints-tutorial/

A deep Belief Network is simply many RBMs stacked one on top of the another. Each hidden layer has a double role: it works as hidden layer to the nodes that come before it, and as input (or visible) layer to the nodes that come after it.

Recently an unsupervised pre-training method gained popularity for initializing deep neural networks with the weights of independent RBMs.

Recurrent networks include a feedback loop, where the output from step $n - 1$ is fed back to the network itself so that this affects the outcome of step n. In this way the network can learn a dynamic model depending on the context of what learned so far.

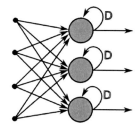

47. What is pre-training?

Solution

Deep Learning has poor performances when trained on random initial weights. In that case a pre-training step is typically adopted, in order to force Deep Network to start in a region of the parameter space, which is close to the zone when a solution is allowed. Pre-training was a key intuition to push the renaissance of Neural Networks after 2006. Before that point the results were very poor.

The key idea is to proceed incrementally. First the lower layers are trained with an unsupervised learning algorithm (generally based on auto-encoders or RBM): the output of each layer is used as pre-trained input for the initialization of the weights of the next layer, one layer after another. Then the whole neural network is fine-tuned by using supervised learning. This two steps approach based on unsupervised training of layer after layer followed by global supervised training has consistently shown to beat random initialization on multiple application domains. There is no clear theoretical explanation of why this happens, but it seems natural to think that the pre-initialization facilitates the finding of a local optima with global supervised techniques such as the Stochastic Gradient Descent.

48. An example of Deep Learning with Nolearn and Lasagne package

Solution

Python has very good support for Deep Learning. In particular, Theano[24] is a Python library that lets you to define, optimize and evaluate mathematical expressions. There are multiple cool features there supported including transparent GPU support and symbolic differentiation, where Theano can automatically build symbolic graphs for computing gradients. On the top of Theano, there is a number of packages which offers Lego-like modules for Deep Learning, including NoLearn[25] and Lasagne[26]. At present these modules are supposed to converge into one common library. Lasagne already supports multiple Deep Learning layers including *Input, Convolutional, Pooling, Recurrent, Noise, Shape, Merge, Embedding* and many others which emerged in the last five years.

The following code takes a classical image dataset coming from MNIST[27] , it splits it into training and test and then trains a Deep Belief Network (DBN) with 784 input nodes – which is the size of a 28x28 grayscale image – , 300 RBN units and 10 output units for a maximum of 10 epochs, a learning rate of 0.3 and a decay of 0.9. Once the network is trained, it can be used for predicting. In a pretty simple way, you just take your lego-like module from Nolearn and train it! Just black magic art!

The second code fragment defines a ConvNet in Lasagne - with multiple layers - it filters and optimizes parameters. Once the network is shaped, training can happen by calling the *fit* method implemented in Lasagne.

---

[24] http://deeplearning.net/software/theano/introduction.html#introduction

[25] https://pythonhosted.org/nolearn/

[26] http://lasagne.readthedocs.org/en/latest/

[27] https://en.wikipedia.org/wiki/MNIST_database

Code

```
# import the necessary packages
from sklearn.cross_validation import train_test_split
from sklearn.metrics import classification_report
from sklearn import datasets
from nolearn.dbn import DBN
import numpy as np
# the MNIST dataset
print "[X] downloading data..."
dataset = datasets.fetch_mldata("MNIST Original")
(trainX, testX, trainY, testY) = train_test_split(
    dataset.data / 255.0,
dataset.target.astype("int0"), test_size = 0.33)

# train the Deep Belief Network with 784 input units
(the flattened,
# 28x28 grayscale image), 300 hidden units, 10 output
units (one for
# each possible output classification, which are the
digits 1-10)
dbn = DBN(
    [trainX.shape[1], 300, 10],
    learn_rates = 0.3,
    learn_rate_decays = 0.9,
    epochs = 10,
    verbose = 1)
dbn.fit(trainX, trainY)
# compute the predictions for the test data and show a
classification
# report
preds = dbn.predict(testX)
print classification_report(testY, preds)
```

Outcome

```
...
Epoch 9:
  loss 0.0238578826697
  err  0.00730020491803
  (0:00:03)
100%
Epoch 10:
  loss 0.0189791078394
  err  0.00512295081967
```

(0:00:04)

	precision	recall	f1-score	support
0	0.98	0.99	0.99	2269
1	0.98	0.99	0.99	2623
2	0.97	0.99	0.98	2323
3	0.98	0.97	0.98	2354
4	0.97	0.98	0.97	2276
5	0.98	0.97	0.97	2004
6	0.98	0.99	0.99	2351
7	0.98	0.98	0.98	2374
8	0.98	0.97	0.97	2279
9	0.98	0.95	0.96	2247
avg / total	0.98	0.98	0.98	23100

Code

```
net2 = NeuralNet(
    layers = [
        ('input', layers.InputLayer),
        ('conv1', layers.Conv2DLayer),
        ('pool1', layers.MaxPool2DLayer),
        ('conv2', layers.Conv2DLayer),
        ('pool2', layers.MaxPool2DLayer),
        ('conv3', layers.Conv2DLayer),
        ('pool3', layers.MaxPool2DLayer),
        ("hidden4", layers.DenseLayer),
        ("output", layers.DenseLayer),
        ],
        #layer parameters:
        input_shape = (None, 1, 32, 32),
        conv1_num_filters = 16, conv1_filter_size = (3,
3), pool1_pool_size = (2,2),
        conv2_num_filters = 32, conv2_filter_size = (2,
2) , pool2_pool_size =  (2,2),
        conv3_num_filters = 64, conv3_filter_size = (2,
2), pool3_pool_size = (2,2),
        hidden4_num_units = 200,
        output_nonlinearity = softmax,
        output_num_units = 10,

        #optimization parameters:
        update = nesterov_momentum,
        update_learning_rate = 0.015,
        update_momentum = 0.9,
        regression = False,
        max_epochs = 5,
```

```
verbose = 1,
)
```

49.Can you compute an embedding with Word2Vec?

Solution

Word2Vec is a class of neural network models that produces one vector for each word in a textual corpus, by encoding semantic information associated to the word. The vectors can be used as features for NLP tasks such as classification, entity detection and resolution, sentiment analysis and tagging. In addition to that, vectors are used to find similar words by using cosine similarity distance. The output of the Word2vec neural net is a vocabulary in which each item has a vector attached to it, which can be served into a deep-learning net or simply probed to detect relationships between words.

One interesting characteristic of word2vec is that this model trains words against other words that are close inside the input text corpus. This is the so-called context of a word. There are two variants of this idea. The first is called continuous bag of words and it uses the context to predict a target word, while the second one is called skip-gram, it is specular and uses a word for predicting a target context. Spark uses the second model.

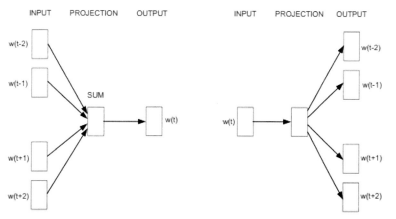

Mathematically the goal is to maximize the average log-likelihood

$$\frac{1}{T}\sum_{t=1}^{T}\sum_{j=-k}^{k} \log p(w_{t+j}|w_t)$$

for T training words in sequence $w_1,...w_T$ and a training window of size k. In the skip-gram model each word has two vectors that are in the representation u_w and the context v_w m while the probability

$$p(w_j|w_t) = \frac{e^{(u_{w_j}^T v_{w_t})}}{\sum_{l=1}^{V} e^{(u_{w_l}^T v_{w_t})}}$$

is expressed via softmax , where V is the vocabulary size. An important aspect of weor2vec is that semantically closer words are mapped into close vectors in the word2vec vector space. In addition those vectors reflect intuitive semantic composition properties as shown in this image.

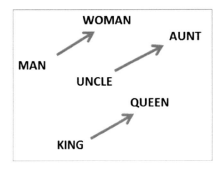
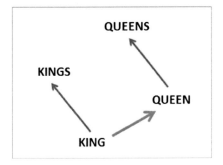

In the first code example, a word2vec model is trained and then similar words to word *china* are retrieved. In the second code example a DataFrame is created containing the text and then a distributed vector representation is computed. Each vector has 10 entries.

Code

```
from pyspark.mllib.feature import Word2Vec

sc = SparkContext()
inp = sc.textFile("text8_lines").map(lambda row:
row.split(" "))

word2vec = Word2Vec()
model = word2vec.fit(inp)
```

```
synonyms = model.findSynonyms('china', 40)

for word, cosine_distance in synonyms:
    print("{}: {}".format(word, cosine_distance))
```

Code

```python
from pyspark import SparkContext
from pyspark.sql import SQLContext
from pyspark.ml.feature import Word2Vec

sc = SparkContext()
sqlContext = SQLContext(sc)
df = sqlContext.createDataFrame([
  ("i still have not found what i am looking
for".split(" "), ),
  ("sense of life is to enjoy the moment".split(" "),
),
  ("if you get an usual mearning of it".split(" "), ),
  ("that witch was close".split(" "), )
], ["text"])
# word2vec.
word2Vec = Word2Vec(vectorSize=10, minCount=0,
inputCol="text", outputCol="result")
model = word2Vec.fit(df)
result = model.transform(df)
for feature in result.select("result").take(4):
  print(feature)
```

50.What are Radial Basis Networks?

Solution

Radial Basis networks are three-layer networks consisting of (a) input nodes connected by weighted edges to (b) a set of proper RBF neurons which fire proportionally to the distance of the input and the activation function and is connected to (c) linear nodes. The activation function is typically a Gaussian and the output layer is simply used to linearly combine all the results of each RBF node. It can be shown that RBN can approximate non-linear functions.

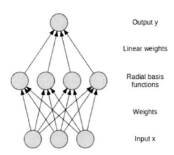

Output y

Linear weights

Radial basis functions

Weights

Input x

Training is made by using a hybrid approach. First each training instance is randomly assigned to a node to initialize the RBN centres, then the perceptron is used to train the output weights. Sometimes the first step is changed by using k-means. The key intuition for RBN is that function approximations are obtained by leveraging the contribution of multiple Gaussians which are activated independently as basis.

Code

Python has a package for implementing RBN named PYRadBas.[28]

51.What are Splines?

Solution

The key idea for Splines is to approximate a function $f(x)$ with a number of polynomial basis $\phi_i(x)$ such as $\phi_0(x) = 1, \ \phi_1(x) = x, \ \phi_2(x) = x^2, \ \phi_3(x) = x^3$

$$f(x) = \sum_i \alpha_i \phi_i(x)$$

such that . Given the basis the problem of approximation is linear and therefore we can fit it with a least square approach.

Code

Python has multiple packages for spline interpolation. For instance, scipy.interpolate has a support to the least square split fit.[29]

---

[28] http://stefano.brilli.me/pyradbas/

[29] http://docs.scipy.org/doc/scipy-0.16.0/reference/generated/scipy.interpolate.splrep.html

52. What are Self-Organized-Maps (SOMs)?

Solution

Self Organized Maps are two-layers networks. The input layer performs no computation and the weights are used only for activation. The SOM layer is fully connected in a square 2-d grid where each activated neuron changes also the state of the other adjacent nodes.

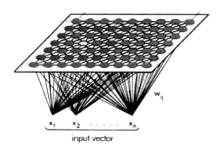

input vector

Mathematically all the neurons are randomly initialized. Then at iteration t the neuron j minimizing the Euclidean distance between the input and the its current weight is selected as winner. The weights of the winner are updated as $w^{t+1}_j = w^t_j + \eta(w^t_j - x)$ where η is the learning rate and x is the input. In addition to that, the weights of the adjacent neurons in the grid map are updated as $w^{t+1}_k = w^t_k + \eta * nb(j,k)(w^t_j - x)$ where $nb(j,k)$ is a neighbour function which decides whether the neuron k is near enough to the winning neuron j in the map. Once the network is trained, a classification can be performed by selecting the best neuron minimizing the Euclidean distance.

Code

Python has a package for implementing SOM named SOMPY.[30]

---

[30] https://github.com/sevamoo/SOMPY

53.What is Conjugate Gradient?

Solution

The Conjugate Gradient (CG) is a method for finding the nearest local minimum of a function of n variables with a known gradient. It uses conjugate directions instead of the local gradient for descending. Frequently the minimum is reached in less steps than one needed by a normal gradient descent.

Suppose that a line minimization along the direction u has been just completed. Then the gradient ∇f at the current point is perpendicular to u, because otherwise it would have been possible to move further along u. Next it should be possible to move along a direction v. In steepest descent this is achieved by letting $v = -\nabla f$. In the conjugate gradient method $-\nabla f$ is perturbed by adding a direction to it to become v. The key idea is to choose v in such a way that it does not undo the minimization along u. In other words, ∇f is required to be perpendicular, at least locally to u, before and after the algorithm moves along v.

In short CG is more expensive than the Gradient Descent but it will generally converge to the local minimum in a faster way. This is represented in the following image where the green line represents the Gradient Descent and the red one the Conjugate Gradient.

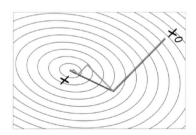

54.What is exploitation-exploration? And what is the armed bandit method?

Solution

Exploitation-Exploration is an adaptive method used for finding the optimal solution in a search space. The idea is to combine an exploration phase where new solutions are tested together with an exploitation phase where the current best solution is used. One way to think about this approach is the so called *n-armed bandit* problem. Suppose to have a room with n armed bandit slot machines. At the beginning the algorithm will explore the room trying to find the machine which pays more – this is the so called exploration phase – but after a while a phase of exploration will be alternated trying to maximize the return on investment for the information acquired so far.

55.What is Simulated Annealing?

Solution

Simulated Annealing is an optimization method derived by Physics. The idea is to describe the problem in terms of temperature T and energy state E. At the beginning the system has an observed state $<T_0, E_0>$. Then the state is randomly perturbated to understand if energy will decrease. If energy is lower, then the new state is accepted in a similar way to Gradient Descent. If not, the new state is still accepted with probability $e^{\frac{E_{t+1}-E_t}{T}}$, where t is the current iteration, which is a heuristic adopted solution to escape from local minima. By every few iteration the annealing schedule is applied by reducing temperature $T_{t+k} = cT_t$ where $0 < c < 1$. The approach is repeated until $T > 0$ or for a maximum number of iterations.

Code

Scipy has a good implementation of the simulated annealing[31] method.

56. What is a Monte Carlo experiment?

Solution

Monte Carlo experiments are a class of algorithms relying on repeated random sampling in order to obtain numerical results such as the estimation of the probability distribution for a variable. For instance, Monte Carlo simulators can be used to assess the risk of a given trading strategy with options or stocks. The basic idea is that if many samples are drawn from a distribution and a histogram is made, the histogram will be shaped similarly the original distribution.

For instance, in a first experiment we simulate the failure rate of working devices knowing that the probability of failure for each of them is $p = 0.000001$. Let us suppose that we have $m = 1000$ devices and we want to know the number of still working devices after $n = 5$ years. The number of failing devices follows a Poisson distribution that can be simulated with a code fragment.

Let's see another example for estimating π. If we have a circle of radius r and this is inscribed in a square with length $2r$ then the area of the circle is πr^2 and the area of the square is $(2r)^2$. Therefore the ratio of the area of the circle to the area of the square will be $\frac{\pi}{4}$. In other words, if we pick n random points, then approximately $n\frac{\pi}{4}$ will follow inside the circle and we can check if a point (x, y) is inside the circle with $x^2 + y^2 < r^2$. If we count how many times a point falls inside the circle (say m), then we can approximate as

$$\pi = \frac{\frac{4m}{n}}{}$$

[31]http://docs.scipy.org/doc/scipy-
0.15.1/reference/generated/scipy.optimize.anneal.html

Code

```python
import numpy as np

n = 1000
m = 5
p = 1.0 / 100000

for _ in range(50):
    failed = np.random.poisson(n * m * p)
    print "Failed %d" %failed


import math
import random
maxIt = 1000000

ctr = 0
for i in range(maxIt):
    if math.pow(random.random(), 2.0) +
math.pow(random.random(), 2.0) <= 1.0:
        ctr += 1

print "PI = ", 4.0 * ctr / maxIt
```

57. What is a Markov Chain?

Solution

A Markov chain is a random process described by means of a direct graph where nodes are states and edges represent the probability to move from one state to another. Transitions are memory-less in the sense that the transition from the current state only depends on that state and not on the previous choices. The stationary distribution of a Markov Chain with transition matrix P is a vector, ψ, such that $\psi P = \psi$. It can be shown that PageRank computation is equivalent to finding the stationary distribution of a suitable matrix.

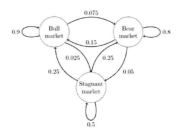

58.What is Gibbs sampling?

Solution

When the conditional probability of each variable is known, it is possible to use Gibbs sampling to infer the joint distribution. Gibbs sampling generates an instance from each variable distribution conditioned in turn on the current values of the other variables inside the distribution itself. It can be thus shown that the stationary distribution of the generated Markov chain is the joint distribution.

For instance, assume that we have pairs (x, y), where x represents the outcome of a first die and y is the sum of the outcome of the first and second die, Gibbs sampling works by starting with any valid value for x and y and then repeatedly alternate replacing x with a random value conditioned to y and y with a random value conditioned on x. After a certain number of iterations x and y will represent a sample from the unconditioned distribution. This code fragment in Python illustrates the method.

Code

```
def roll_a_die():
    return random.choice([1,2,3,4,5,6])

def random_y_given_x(x):
    return x+roll_a_die()

def random_x_given_y(y):
    if y<=7
        return random.randomrange(1,y)
    else
        return random.randomrange(y-6,7)

def gibbSampling(numIters=200):
    x=0,1
```

```
for _ in range(numIters):
    x=random_x_given_y(y)
    y=random_y_given_x(x)
return x, y
```

59. What is Locality Sensitive Hashing (LSH)?

Solution

Locality-sensitive hashing (LSH) reduces the dimensionality of high-dimensional data. LSH hashes items so that similar items map to the same hashed value with high probability. This is quite different from cryptographic hashing, where the goal is to map objects to numbers with a low collision rate and high randomness. In order to achieve this goal, there are multiple ways to hash data and this subject is matter of intensive studies.

Here we propose only one approach and the interested reader can refer to the link below[32] for a more extensive discussion. The key idea is that without losing in generality data can be represented by d-dimensional vectors in $\{0, 1\}^d$. Then a random function simply selects a random bit from the input point. More sophisticate hash functions can be also used.

Python has multiple packages for LSH computation. One of them is LSHash[33], which is very easy to use.

Code

```
from lshash import LSHash

lsh = LSHash(hash_size=6, input_dim=8)
lsh.index([1,2,3,4,5,6,7,8])
lsh.index([2,3,4,5,6,7,8,9])
lsh.index([10,12,99,1,5,31,2,3
# returns the closer vectors in the hashed space
print lsh.query([1,2,3,4,5,6,7,7])
```

---

[32] https://en.wikipedia.org/wiki/Locality-sensitive_hashing

[33] https://github.com/kayzh/LSHash

60. What is minHash?

Min Hash permutation is a rather sophisticate hashing function which can be used for LSH. The idea is that given a set of items S and a subset U and supposing to use Jaccard index J as similarity function, it is possible to compute J with minHash permutation. Given two sets A, B the

$$J(A, B) = \frac{|A \cap B|}{|A \cup B|}$$

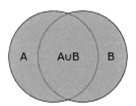

Mathematically let π be a permutation of the index of S and let $h(A) = \min\limits_{a \in A} \{ \pi(a) \}$ be the minimum permutation for $A \subseteq S$. It can be shown that with this definition an important propriety will hold $P[h(A) = h(B)] = J(A,B)$. In other words the min permutation allows us to compute efficiently the jaccard similarity index between input data items.

Python has a nice implementation of minHash[34] and the following code fragment uses it.

Code

```
from hashlib import sha1
from datasketch import MinHash

data1 = ['minhash', 'is', 'a', 'probabilistic', 'data',
'structure', 'for',
        'estimating', 'the', 'similarity', 'between',
'datasets']
data2 = ['minhash', 'is', 'a', 'probability', 'data',
'structure', 'for',
        'estimating', 'the', 'similarity', 'between',
'documents']
```

---

[34] https://github.com/ekzhu/datasketch

```
m1, m2 = MinHash(), MinHash()
for d in data1:
    m1.digest(sha1(d.encode('utf8')))
for d in data2:
    m2.digest(sha1(d.encode('utf8')))
print("Estimated Jaccard for data1 and data2 is",
m1.jaccard(m2))

s1 = set(data1)
s2 = set(data2)
actual_jaccard =
float(len(s1.intersection(s2)))/float(len(s1.union(s2))
)
print("Actual Jaccard for data1 and data2 is",
actual_jaccard)
```

61.What are Bloom Filters?

Solution

A Bloom filter is a probabilistic data structure that, given a set of elements S, can be used to understand if an element is definitely not in S or if it's highly probable to find it in the set. The key idea is that the Bloom filter is a compact hashed data structure that allows to rapidly check if an element is not in S in a deterministic way and at the same time it allows to rapidly check if an element is in S with few cases of false positives.

Python has many modules for implementing Bloom Filters. For instance, pybloom is used in the following code fragment.

Code

```
from pybloom import BloomFilter
f = BloomFilter(capacity=1000, error_rate=0.001)
[f.add(x) for x in range(10)]
[False, False, False, False, False, False, False,
False, False, False]
print all([(x in f) for x in range(10)])
```

62.What is Count Min Sketches?

Solution

Count Min Sketches is an efficient technique used for approximate counting over a stream of data. (*An improved data stream summary: the count-min sketch and its applications in: Journal of Algorithms, 2005, pp. 58-75., "G. Cormode and S. Muthukrisnan")*

Suppose for instance that there is the need of counting the number of page views that a web page receives over a stream that comprises many thousands of URLs per second. Even simple operations such as maintaining counters can be too expensive. In those situations count-min sketches can help because computational requirements for counting are drastically reduced in exchange of some accuracy.

Python has many packages for implementing count min sketches

Code

```
from countminsketch import CountMinSketch
sketch = CountMinSketch(1000, 10)   # table size=1000,
hash functions=10
sketch.add("this")
sketch.add("this")
print sketch["this"]
```

63.How to build a news clustering system

Solution

News clustering is a hard problem to be solved. News articles are typically arriving to our clustering engine in a continuous streaming fashion. Therefore a plain vanilla batch approach is not feasible. For instance the simple idea of using k-means cannot work for two reasons. First, it is not possible to know the number of clusters a-priori because the topics are dynamically evolving. Second, the articles themselves are not available a-priori. Therefore more sophisticate strategies are required.

One initial idea is to split data in mini-batches (perhaps processed with Spark Streaming) and to cluster the content of each mini-batch independently. Then clusters of different epochs (e.g. mini-batches) can be chained together.

An additional intuition is to start with k-seeds and then extend those initial k-clusters whenever a new article that is not similar enough to the initial groups arrives. In this way new clusters are dynamically created when needed. In one additional variant we could think about re-clustering all the articles after a certain number of epochs under the assumption that this will improve our target metric.

In addition to that we can have a look to data and perhaps notice that many articles are near-duplicates. Hence we could aim at reducing the computational complexity by applying pseudo-linear techniques such as minHash shingling.

More sophisticate methods aim at ranking the articles by importance. This is an even harder problem again because of the dynamic nature of the content and the absence of links, which could have allowed PageRank-type computations. If that is not possible, then a two-layer model could be considered where the significance of a news article depends on the importance of the originating news sources, which in turns depends on the importance of the emitted articles. It can be proven that this recurrent definition has a fixed-point solution (*see Ranking a stream of news, WWW '05 Proceedings of the 14th international conference on World Wide Web, Gulli et al.*).

Even more sophisticate methods can aim at extracting entities from the clusters and this is typically achieved by running a topic model detection on the evolving mini-batches.

64.What is A/B testing?

Solution

A/B testing (sometimes called split testing) is comparing two versions of a web page to see which one performs better. The key idea is to compare the two web pages by showing the two variants (named A and B) to similar users at the same time. The variant showing better impact in terms of metric is considered the winner. In jargon the A/B test experiments are called 'flights'.

A certain number of aspects requires attention. First it is important to define a target metric that is tracked for the flight. Then it is important to define how much traffic the flight will receive, the so-called power of the flight (say 10% for A and 10% for B, and the remaining part is devoted to unchanged experience). In addition to that it is important to compute how long the experiment should run for having enough sensitiveness in moving the metric. In turn this depends on the power of the flight and on the metric itself. Moreover it is important to check the validity of the experiment by requiring that the probability for a result to happen by chance is above a given threshold called "significance level". Before the test is performed, the significance level of the test (also known as p-value) is typically set at 5% or 1% for all the modern lean online developments.

The key intuition behind the test is that we believe that our experiment is good, if it is very unlikely that a naïve model (also known as null hypothesis) could perform as well as our experiment. The interested reader can find more information including technical details like the confidence interval as well as practical suggestions to run the experiments in the article: *"Practical guide to controlled experiments on the web, Proceedings of the 13th ACM SIGKDD international conference on Knowledge discovery and data mining, Ron Kohavi et al."*

65.What is Natural Language Processing?

Solution

Natural Language Processing (NLP) is a complex topic and there are books devoted only to this subject. In this book an introductive survey will be provided based on the NLTK, a Python Natural Language Toolkit. Let us start.

A text is made up of *sentences* and sentences are composed of *words*. So the first step in NLP is frequently used to separate those basic units according to the rules of the chosen language. Often very frequent words carry little information and they should be filtered out as *stopwords*. The first code fragment splits the text into sentences and then sentences into words, where stop words are then removed.

In addition to that, it could be interesting to find out the meaning of words and here Wordnet[35] can help with its organization of terms into *synsets,* which are organized into inheritance trees, where the most abstract terms

---

[35] https://wordnet.princeton.edu/

are hypernyms and the more specific terms are hyponyms. Wordnet can also help in finding *synonyms* and *antonyms* (opposite words) of a given term. The code fragment finds the synonyms of the word *love* in English.

Moreover words can be stemmed and the rules for stemming are very different from language to language. NLTK supports the SnowballStemmer that supports multiple idioms. The code fragment finds the stem of the word *volvi* in Spanish.

In certain situations it could be convenient to understand whether a word is a noun, an adjective, a verb and so on. This is the process of part-of-speech tagging and NLTK provides a convenient support for this type of analysis as illustrated in the code fragment below.

Code

```
import nltk.data

text = "Poetry is the record of the best and happiest
moments \
of the happiest and best minds. Poetry is a sword of
lightning, \
ever unsheathed, which consumes the scabbard that would
contain it."

# download stopwords
#nltk.download("stopwords")
from nltk.corpus import stopwords
stop = stopwords.words('english')

# download the punkt package
#nltk.download('punkt')
# load the sentences' tokenizer
tokenizer =
nltk.data.load('tokenizers/punkt/english.pickle')
sentences = tokenizer.tokenize(text)
print sentences

# tokenize in words
from nltk.tokenize import WordPunctTokenizer
tokenizer = WordPunctTokenizer()
for sentence in sentences:
    words = tokenizer.tokenize(sentence)
    words = [w for w in words if w not in stop]
```

```
    print words

#wordnet
#nltk.download("wordnet")
from nltk.corpus import wordnet
for i,j in enumerate(wordnet.synsets('love')):
    print "Synonyms:", ", ".join(j.lemma_names())

# SnowBallStemmer
from nltk.stem import SnowballStemmer
stemmer = SnowballStemmer('spanish')
print "Spanish stemmer"
print stemmer.stem('volver')

#tagger
#nltk.download('treebank')
from nltk.tag import UnigramTagger
from nltk.corpus import treebank
trainSenteces = treebank.tagged_sents()[:5000]
tagger = UnigramTagger(trainSenteces)
tagged = tagger.tag(words)
print tagged
```

Outcome

```
['Poetry is the record of the best and happiest moments
of the happiest and best minds.', 'Poetry is a sword of
lightning, ever unsh
eathed, which consumes the scabbard that would contain
it.']
['Poetry', 'record', 'best', 'happiest', 'moments',
'happiest', 'best', 'minds', '.']
['Poetry', 'sword', 'lightning', ',', 'ever',
'unsheathed', ',', 'consumes', 'scabbard', 'would',
'contain', '.']
Synonyms: love
Synonyms: love, passion
Synonyms: beloved, dear, dearest, honey, love
Synonyms: love, sexual_love, erotic_love
Synonyms: love
Synonyms: sexual_love, lovemaking, making_love, love,
love_life
Synonyms: love
Synonyms: love, enjoy
Synonyms: love
```

```
Synonyms: sleep_together, roll_in_the_hay, love,
make_out, make_love, sleep_with, get_laid, have_sex,
know, do_it, be_intimate, have
_intercourse, have_it_away, have_it_off, screw, fuck,
jazz, eff, hump, lie_with, bed, have_a_go_at_it, bang,
get_it_on, bonk
Spanish stemmer
volv
[('Poetry', None), ('sword', None), ('lightning',
None), (',', u','), ('ever', u'RB'), ('unsheathed',
None), (',', u','), ('consumes
', None), ('scabbard', None), ('would', u'MD'),
('contain', u'VB'), ('.', u'.')]
```

66. Where to go from here

The best next step is to start playing with real data and applying the algorithms presented in this volume. Kaggle[36] is a platform for data prediction in competitions. Companies, organizations and researchers post their data and have it scrutinized by the best experts worldwide. Therefore you can go there and run few competitions for showcasing your value!

Remember: Every problem is represented by means of observed data. Data is noisy. So you need to select the right summaries via feature engineering along with the appropriate algorithm for learning. At the same time it is certainly useful to provide a good mathematical formulation to the machine learning problem. Then it is a matter of training (for supervised learning) and evaluation. For supervised learning a good gold set can help. The process is iterative: when you reach satisfying results or when you are stuck and do not make any progress, that is exactly the right moment for iterating and improving, trying to refine and frequently re-assess all the choices made so far. After a few iterations you might be satisfied of your results and deploy the model online for making forecasts on real unseen data. Users will provide you with feedback (either explicit or implicit) and those are new signals that you might want to collect for further refining your models.

Also remember: : great machine learning results can be achieved by finding the right mix among the steps described in the image below.

---

[36] **https://www.kaggle.com/**

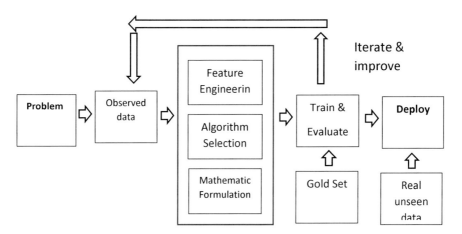

A great Data scientist always works in incremental and lean way!!!

I hope that this second volume provided you with some advanced tools for machine learning and also reduced the halo of mystery surrounding the role of Data science (after all it is all about data, math, coding and lots of creativity!). Now you have a better understanding of multiple learning techniques including linear learners, support vectors, different clustering algorithms, decision trees, random forests, mars, gradient boosted trees, ensembles, hyper-parameters searches, density estimations, expectation-maximizations, dimensional reductions, bagging, recommendations, neural networks, deep learning and associative rules. These are the ingredients of you next machine learning recipe. Now it is up to you. Go and prepare your next delicious machine learning dish!

Appendix A

67.Ultra-Quick introduction to Python

I assume that you are already familiar with programming languages and hopefully you already have some experience with Python. However it is useful to recall some peculiarities of the languages which are used in this book.

Python does not use { } for delimiting code blocks but instead it uses indentation, which can be confusing at the beginning if you are used to C/C++ programming. Importing a module and defining a function have a simple syntax

```
import numpy as np

def dist(p0, p1):
    return np.sum((p0-p1)**2)
```

Lists are defined with square brackets and slicing operations are easily supported.

```
l=[1,2,3,4,5]

x[:3] #first three
x[3:] #three to end
x[2:4] #2nd, 3rd, 4th
y = x[:] #copy
```

List comprehension is useful for transforming a list into another list by selecting some elements or by transforming other elements with a suitable function. This example creates a list of 100 tuples $[(0, 0), (0,1), ... (100, 100)]$

```
pairs = [(x, y) for x in range(10) for y in range(10)]
```

Python supports anonymous functions also known as lambda computation. This is frequently used in Spark as reported in this example:

```
# map reduce
```

```
textFile.map(lambda line: len(line.split())).reduce(lambda a, b: a if (a > b) else b)
```

Numpy is a library for efficient linear algebra and numerical computation. In this book we used numpy vectors intensively.

```
import numpy as np

def dist(p0, p1):
    return np.sum((p0-p1)**2)

def knn(training, trainingLabels, newPoint):
    dists = np.array([distance(t, newPoint)] for t in training)
    nearest = dists.argmin()
    return trainingLabels[nearest]
```

Anaconda is a very convenient Python distribution for Data Science.[37]

68. Ultra-Quick introduction to Probabilities

Probabilities can be seen as a way to quantify uncertainty for an event E from a universe of events. Mathematically this is denoted with $P(E)$. Two events E, F are independent, if the probability of having both of them happening is $P(E, F) = P(E)P(F)$. If the events are not independent, then $(E, F) = P(E \mid F)P(F)$, which means that the joint probability is equal to the conditional probability of seeing E given F, times the probability of F.

The Bayes theorem is a powerful tool for learning because it allows to *reverse* conditional probabilities. Mathematically the theorem states that:

$$P(E \mid F) = \frac{P(E, F)}{P(F)} \underset{Bayes}{=} \frac{P(F \mid E)P(E)}{P(F)}$$

---

[37] https://store.continuum.io/cshop/anaconda/

69. Ultra-Quick introduction to Matrices and Vectors

Vectors of length n represent points in an n-dimensional space. Vectors are typically represented with the notation x_i with $i = 1,...,n$ and sometimes with bold letters x when there is no ambiguity. Matrices are tables with rows and columns. They are typically represented as $A_{i,j}$ and when there is no ambiguity as **A**. The transpose of a matrix $A_{i,j}$ is $A_{j,i}$ and it is denoted as A^T. The transpose of a vector x of dimension n × 1 is the same vector 1 × n.

Given a vector **x,** we define the norm $$||x||_p = (\sum_{i=1}^{n} |x_i|^p)^{\frac{1}{p}}$$ and $||x||_\infty = max(|x_1|, ..., |x_n|)$

Given two vectors $x,$ **y,** the inner product is $$x\,y = \sum_{i=1}^{n} x_i y_i$$. Given the inner product, we define the cosine similarity as $$\cos(\theta) = \frac{xy}{(xx)(yy)} = \frac{xy}{||x||\,||y||},$$ where θ is the angle between the vectors represented by x and y.

Given two vectors **x, y,** the outer product $x \otimes y$ is equivalent to a matrix multiplication xy^T, provided that x is represented as a $m \times 1$ column vector and y as an n × 1 column vector.

$$a \otimes b = ab^T = \begin{bmatrix} a_1 b_1 & \cdots & a_1 b_n \\ \vdots & \ddots & \vdots \\ a_n b_1 & \cdots & a_n b_n \end{bmatrix}$$

Given a square matrix A, a non-zero vector v is said eigenvector of A if the following relation holds:

$$Av = \lambda v$$

For a given scalar $\lambda > 0$

70.Ultra-Quick summary of metrics

In this section a summary of the main metrics used in different machine learning tasks is presented.

Classification Metrics

Name	Formula
Accuracy	$$\frac{TP + TN}{TP + TN + FN + FP}$$
Precision	$$\frac{TP}{TP + FP}$$
Recall	$$\frac{TP}{TP + FN}$$
Specificity	$$\frac{TN}{TN + FP}$$
F1	$$\frac{2 * precision * recall}{precision + recall}$$
ROC (Receiver Operating Characteristic)	A plot representing the percentage of true positives in the y-axis and the percentage of true negatives in the x-axis
AUC (Area Under the Curve)	Used to summarize the bi-dimensional ROC into a single value represented by the area under the ROC curve. The higher the value the merrier
Recall-precision curve	A plot representing the recall in the y-axis and the precision in the x-asis

Where TP are true positives, TN are true negatives, FP are false positives , and FN are false negatives. Note that the precision is the number of documents that are relevant over the total number of relevant documents. Instead the recall is the number of documents retrieved that are relevant over the total number of retrieved documents.

Clustering Metrics

Name	Formula
Intra-cluster distance	Maximum distance between any pair of elements in the cluster
Inter-cluster distance	Maximum distance between any cluster

Scoring Metrics

Name	Formula
RMSE	$\sqrt{\dfrac{1}{N}\sum\limits_{i=1}^{N}(prediction_i - actual_i)^2}$
MSE	$\dfrac{1}{N}\sum\limits_{i=1}^{N}(prediction_i - actual_i)^2$
R-squared	$\dfrac{1 - \sum\limits_{i=1}^{N}(prediction_i - actual_i)^2}{\dfrac{1}{N}\sum\limits_{i=1}^{N}(prediction_i - actual_i)^2}$
Mean Absolute	$\dfrac{1}{N}\sum\limits_{i=1}^{N}|(prediction_i - actual_i)|$

Rank Correlation Metrics

Name	Formula

Kendall	$\tau = \dfrac{1}{0.5n(n-1)} * [(number\ of\ conco\ $
Person	$\rho_{xy} = \dfrac{cov(x,y)}{var(x)var(y)}$ where x, y are the ranks
Spearman	$\rho = 1 - \dfrac{6\sum(x_i - y_i)^2}{n(n^2 - 1)}$ where x, y are the ranks

Probability Metrics

Name	Formula
Log-likelihood	The likelihood of a set of parameter values, θ, given outcomes x, is equal to the probability of those observed outcomes given those parameter values. In short, $L(\theta \mid x) = P(x \mid \theta)$. In many applications is more convenient to use the logarithms
Entropy	$H(X) = -\sum P(x_i) log P(x_i)$
Cross-Entropy	$H(X,Y) = -\sum P(x_i) log P(y_i)$

Ranking Models

Name	Formula
DCG (discounted cumulative gain)	$rel_1 + \sum_{i=2}^{p} \dfrac{rel_i}{log^{[m]}(i)}$, where rel_i is the vote for position i

| NDCG | Sort the documents and produce the maxium DCG till position p (ideal DCG for position p, $IDCG_p$) $$NDCG_p = \frac{DCG_p}{IDCG_p}$$ |

71. Comparison of different machine learning techniques

In this section some takeaways are summarized

Linear regression

- Linear regression is always the starting point for modelling quantities
- As the name says, this methodology is particularly useful for linear separable datasets, which is frequently the case for very high dimensions (e.g. when the number of features is very high).
- Regularization can provide sparse sets of weights and it is always recommended to fine tune hyper-parameters related to L1-norm, L2-norm or ElasticNet.
- Training can be considered in terms of residuals. It starts with the variable which best correlates with the error and then iteratively the residuals are minimized.
- Linear regression is very efficient in providing the output, it simply consists in a vector multiplication.
- Some forms of feature selection are always recommended as well as combinations of multiple features and transformation.
- However linear regression does not work well when the data is not linearly separable.

Logistic regression

- Logistic regression is the starting point for binary classification.
- Logistic regression can map real numbers into probabilities.

- However logistic regression might have problems with a very large number of variables, or with categorical variables with a very large number of outputs.

Support Vector Machines

- Support vectors can be used on linear separable data.
- Kernel methods can be used to map data into a space where data is linearly separable (they can also be used in regression and in any other linear method).

Clustering

- Clustering is an unsupervised learning technique about how to group similar items together.
- Different types of similarity functions can be defined.
- Clustering might be used for data exploration, outliers detection or for final products.
- However clustering is essentially based on heuristics and a rigorous methodology for evaluation must be always provided.

Decision Trees, Random Forests, and GBTs

- Decision trees are the out-of-the box machine learning techniques.
- The models built by Decision Trees are very intuitive and simple to understand.
- Decision trees typically work with categorical variables but can be adopted to numerical ones.
- However, decision trees might overfit data and once a splitting choice is made, it cannot be reverted.
- Bagging reduces variance and can reduce problems in generalization.
- Random forests use bagging to allow multiple choices when the sequences of trees are built. Each tree improves the error observed by the previous ones.
- However Random forests can be still overfit because are typically deep and unpruned. Cross-validation might help as usual.
- Gradient boosted trees build multiple trees in parallel and multiple splitting choices can be made in each different tree.
- All those methods work well with non-linearly separable data.

Associative Rules

- Associative rules are useful for finding correlations in data in which items tends to occur together.
- However it is important to use modern methods for finding frequent itemsets such as FP-Growth.

Neural Networks and Deep Learning

- Neural networks are popular for many learning tasks including classification, compression and regression. Neural Networks have multiple successful applications such as image processing, speech recognition, npl and others.
- Recent algorithmic progress made possible to revamp the interest in neural networks because it is now possible to train larger networks. Also pre-training showed significant improvements in many disciplines adopting Neural Networks.
- GPUs processing made possible to build deep networks made by many more layers.
- Parallel computation and Spark-like frameworks made possible to build very large scale platforms for Deep learning with dozens of cpus.
- However, GPU and Parallel computation are still two separate fields at the end of 2015
- Deep Learning made it possible to have Trainable feature extractors in addition to Trainable learners. The latter are essentially learning an optimal weight for manually handcrafted features. The former can select the right weights on user's behalf.
- However the optimal composition of Neural network layers is still requiring a lot of manual effort and it is more of less a black magic art based on a lot of try-failure-success manual efforts.
- Learning how to compose the layers is most likely the Big step for Datascience.

ABOUT THE AUTHOR

An experienced data mining engineer, passionate about technology and innovation in consumers' space. Interested in search and machine learning on massive dataset with a particular focus on query analysis, suggestions, entities, personalization, freshness and universal ranking. Antonio Gulli has worked in small startups, medium (Ask.com, Tiscali) and large corporations (Microsoft, RELX). His carrier path is about mixing industry with academic experience.

Antonio holds a Master Degree in Computer Science and a Master Degree in Engineering, and a Ph.D. in Computer Science. He founded two startups, one of them was one of the earliest search engine in Europe back in 1998. He filed more than 20 patents in search, machine learning and distributed system. Antonio wrote several books on algorithms and currently he serves as (Senior) Program Committee member in many international conferences. Antonio teaches also computer science and video game programming to hundreds of youngsters on a voluntary basis.

"Nowadays, you must have a great combination of research skills and a just-get-it-done attitude."

34012142R00061

Made in the USA
Middletown, DE
04 August 2016